Where Does Autism Come From?

The Theory of "Almost I"

Cooper R. Woodard, PhD, BCBA

Contents

Preface and Acknowledgements

Introduction: What Is Autism, Really?   3

Chapter 1: Early Infancy and the Core Symptoms   9

Chapter 2: What We Know About Genes,   21
      Environment, and Treatment

Chapter 3: Typical Early Development and the   35
      Emergence of Imagination

Chapter 4: The Real Victims in Autism: Imagination,   59
      Symbolism, and Pretend Play

Chapter 5: One Way to Explain It: Identification   76

Chapter 6: Identification with Inanimate Objects: The   91
      Absence of "I"

Chapter 7: The Identification Continuum and Emergence   107
      of "I"

Chapter 8: Yes, There Is Research to Support These Ideas!   124

Chapter 9: How Technology May Be at the Root of Autism   143

Chapter 10: Treatment Ideas and Implications for Society   156

Final Thoughts   176

References   177

Preface and Acknowledgements

The main purpose of this book is to demonstrate and explain how autism is an altered early trajectory of the development of an essential feature of mature, human thinking—the ability to think "about" or imagine, in the broadest sense of the word. This particular thinking ability is in itself, essential to understanding the main points contained in this volume. To be able to understand what autism is, the reader will need to imagine what it is like *not to be able to imagine*. This is not an easy task for everyone who comes in contact with these ideas, mainly because this ability is such a core feature of who and what we are as thinking humans. We employ this ability with such ease and regularity as adults, that imagining what it is like *not to be able to imagine* is difficult.

This book is an expansion of an article that I had published in 2011. While I was able to outline some of the main ideas in that article, space limitations did not allow for full explanations. Since those limits do not presently exist, we will begin with a discussion of what the diagnosis of autism actually entails, and more importantly, discuss the many symptoms not technically included in a diagnosis. These associated symptoms provide some essential clues to understanding autism, and will be returned to later in the book.

Next, we will discuss the many fruitless attempts to identify the cause of autism, as well as the few basic facts we do currently have. This will lead us directly into a presentation of our core concepts and thesis, the development of early imaginative capacities that derive from the psychoanalytic process of part- to whole-object identification and internalization. Because this process is a multifaceted and complex one, we will need to

1

consider the various sources of potential influence from both genetic and environmental sources. We will then discuss a range of research findings that support this theory.

Finally, with these concepts understood, we can begin to speculate on why rates of this disorder appear to be increasing. One factor influencing the increasing rate of autism comes from trends within our own culture: technological, non-personal engagement that is fueling a subtle change in who we are, how we think and behave, how we interact with our infants, and perhaps the thinking predispositions of our children.

My sincerest thanks to my partner John Neill, my sister Camaron, and my parents Ralph and Carol for listening to my endless discussions on this topic.

Cooper R. Woodard

Introduction

What Is Autism, Really?

Autism is not an easy diagnosis to make. The reality is that the symptoms don't appear in an easily recognizable form, which means they can be easy to miss, vary in intensity, and change over time. Sometimes a child seems fine until around age 2 and sometimes not. Testing, when it's available, is complex to administer and difficult to score. Sometimes people with autism can speak and sometimes they cannot, and cognitive skills can vary widely from one person to the next. These challenges make autism more difficult to diagnose than other disorders such as attention deficit disorder (ADD) or depression. When speaking of autism, you may hear clinicians say, "You'll know it when you see it," because trying to describe a condition this variable, complicated, and disjointed is extremely challenging, if not nearly impossible.

Traditionally, autism has been made up of a set of three subcategories that do not fit together in any comprehensive or meaningful way: Social impairments, communication impairments, and repetitive behaviors. While there are these general diagnostic criteria, the symptoms just don't go together in any way that is inherently familiar to the typically developing person. For example, when someone is anxious, it doesn't come as a surprise that they are nervous, jittery, and may have trouble focusing. These symptoms are familiar and part of our understanding of what it means to be anxious. Similarly, depression is relatively straight-forward; you feel sad, not interested in things that used to be interesting, tired, and probably have trouble eating and/or sleeping. We can identify with this grouping of symptoms, having most likely felt some form or another of depression at certain points in our lives.

"If you know one person with autism, you know one person with autism."

But autism is very different. It doesn't happen as a result of a series of life events, it doesn't go away, there are no medications that effectively treat the core symptoms (yet), and the subcategories don't really form one unique, coherent whole with which most people could identify. We don't have a clear understanding about how it happens, where it comes from, or what can be done to prevent it. Because of this reality, most people don't have a very good understanding of autism or its diagnosis until they are forced to deal with it if/when it touches their life, which is happening more and more frequently these days. People seem to have a sense that autism is not something they want for their children. Upon hearing that I work with children and young adults on the autism spectrum, people often say something like, "You must be a very special person to work with children like that." But my response is always the same; these are people without malice, shame, or most of the less desirable traits that are typically part of the human experience. They are, in fact, a joy to spend time with, and in some ways set an excellent example for the rest of us "typically developing" people.

This book is an attempt to lessen some of the mystery that surrounds autism. Having worked with people with autism and other developmental disabilities for nearly 25 years, I have come to appreciate the varied presentations of autism (and there are many), as well as the courage, suffering, resilience, fear, strength, and other traits and emotions that this diagnosis can elicit from persons with this disorder, as well as from their families. I had an atypical combination of behavioral and psychoanalytic training, which has been essential to my understanding of autism. While some might see these two perspectives as diametrically opposed to one another, I consider them complementary—and the key to unraveling autism, one of the most complex and problematic psychological disorders of our time.

To better understand autism, we will begin by defining it as best we can. This means not only looking at standard diagnostic criteria, but also any associated features that represent the clues and hints about what autism really is that have been scattered about. As I have stated, autism has many different presentations and one often hears the statement, "If you know one person with autism, you know one person with autism." So, we will start with how we currently conceive of autism, and then we will discuss what we know about where autism comes from and what treatments help. But more importantly, we will also discuss what we don't know, which is a lot. We'll begin in Chapter 1 by looking at early infancy and the core symptoms of autism in the context of typical early indicators, as well as some notable and unusual events that can take place that are possible contributing factors of autism. In Chapter 2, we will discuss what we know about the origins and treatment of autism. There has been a lot of effort made to identify the gene(s) responsible for autism, as well as the environmental factors or "toxins" that may be fueling this disorder. The fruits of this research provide more clues to what autism is—and what it is not.

The ability to *think about*

Chapters 3 and 4 require you to put on an abstract thinking cap because you will have to try to imagine what it is like *to not be able to imagine*, a cognitive skill that is part and parcel of who you are and how you think. We will start by considering what typically happens around 1 to 2 years of age that creates the human ability to *think about* the world around us, drawing on a number of theorist's ideas. Most people don't realize that your thinking typically changes in a really significant way at this young age, and that you develop a much more sophisticated way of understanding and interacting with the world. In other words, you really don't come equipped at birth with the ability to *think about* or to imagine. This

5

ability is something that has to emerge and usually it just happens automatically, and no one really considers how significant a change this is when it is happening. There are a number of alternate terms to explain this concept of *thinking about*, but the main idea is "duality of thinking", that there is the object and also the symbol of the object, the actual reality and the imagined reality; and there is direct thinking and *thinking about* thinking. This skill allows you to do a lot of things early in life, like imagine things, lie, be coy, understand the symbols that create communication, and engage in pretend play. This ability helps you as you age and without it, a number of things that typically happen as you get older simply do not happen. This *thinking about* idea is not new and is called "meta-cognition" or "meta-representation," and it is the basic idea behind the well-known "theory of mind" (ToM) concept.

Once you understand what is supposed to happen, of course you will want to understand how it happens and what the result might be if it doesn't happen. This takes a bit of explaining, and in Chapters 5, 6, and 7 we will consider the many ways in which developmental processes might be affected or altered from a psychoanalytic perspective, resulting at times in the outcome of autism. The main idea here is pretty simple: to be able to develop the ability to *think about*, a toddler needs to identify or "link up" psychologically and cognitively with another person. If the toddler links up with something else that is not a person, that will affect his or her ability to *think about*. What you identify with and the extent to which you identify with it determines how you are able to think. Variations to this process are what creates autism, and in Chapter 7, we discuss how these variations in identification explain why a "spectrum" of disorder has emerged. This theory explains pretty much everything we know about autism, which up to this point has not been explained in any understandable way. Our theory explains many apparently disjointed aspects of autism: A conglomerate of symptoms, why autism tends to emerge around age 2, why persons with autism tend to think in rigid and mechanistic ways, and even why there are so many variations of this disorder.

Cause and effect: Psychological disorders typically don't emerge in a bubble

Once we review a bit of the research that supports these ideas in Chapter 8, we will shift gears to discuss a purely hypothetical proposal. If we are proposing that to varying degrees identification with objects instead of people leads to autism, and we know there are more and more cases of autism emerging, then what is causing the increase in identification with objects? It is important to understand that psychological disorders, or any set of traits, don't emerge in a bubble. They are typically a function of a complex interplay between genetics and cultural patterns and environmental conditions. Autism is no different and our hypothetical proposal is that the increasing prevalence of autism in developed countries is directly related to our continually increasing interaction with objects and resulting decreasing need to interact socially with each other, as well as societal rewards for being good at interacting with objects. To better understand our hypothetical proposal, we will discuss this idea in Chapter 9 along with a disorder that may seem completely unrelated: anorexia. The reason for this is that anorexia provides a very good example of how a culture can nearly create and fuel the emergence of a psychological disorder. We know this because anorexia did not always exist and is not present in all cultures.

What would happen if large groups of people increasingly and over decades looked more at machines than they do at each other, and then had children who were trained from an early age to do the same thing? What would happen if you kept repeating that trend or process over and over, continually increasing the proportion of object focus versus people focus? I would suggest that autism is the obvious result. If a culture moves in the direction of object engagement, the tendency will be for parents to be less socially adept, and for infants to have a natural predisposition to be more drawn to objects than to people. If you put those two things together over and over, it only makes sense that the child would tend to identify with objects more often. From here, the next question you need to ask is, what can be done about it? In our final chapter, Chapter 10, we will discuss that very question and the development of the Meta-play Method an autism intervention set I developed following my theoretical paper of 2010. I conducted a pilot study that was published in 2014, and then a small group feasibility study in 2018. Additional research on this method by researchers other than myself is ongoing. The Meta-play Method is based on the idea that the roots of autism lie in a child's early development, and involve a chosen identification with objects instead of people. It follows then that treatment involves bringing the very young child back to people, so that appropriate cognitive development can progress. This is what we do in the activities of the Meta-play Method and it is not an easy task, but we have had some initial promising results.

As you can see, we have a lot to cover, so let's get started.

Chapter 1: Early Infancy and Core Symptoms

Before we discuss the core symptoms of autism and the criteria used to make the diagnosis in a young child, adolescent, or adult, we will look at some of the typical early indicators of autism that researchers have found. In very early infancy, there are some distinct, notable, and unusual events that can take place. For example, parents of infants often report extremes of temperament, poor eye contact, and a lack of response to the parent's play attempts (Zwaigenbaum et al., 2005). This doesn't happen all the time, but it certainly does happen, which suggests that what the newborn brings into the world may be present from birth, or may not. Infants later diagnosed with autism typically lack facial expression and they do not smile socially, respond to their name being called, or orient to faces. These young infants lack spontaneous imitation, and can have abnormal muscle tone. Zwaigenbaum further suggests that it's not until 12 months of age or older that an autism diagnosis could be predicted; behaviors at age 6 months simply do not predict a later diagnosis. Typically developing infants, on the other hand, are more and more able to disengage quickly from a visually perceived object in the environment.

It is important to keep in mind that these researchers' predictive behaviors (in addition to those already listed) include a socially disinterested early temperament followed by later extreme distress reactions and poor visual tracking associated with an increasing inability to disengage from visual stimuli. Simply put, Zwaigenbaum found that very young infants who were later diagnosed with autism did not actively engage with their environment in a number of ways. While this may sound somewhat harmless—and in many situations may, in fact, be harmless—such non-activity is associated with serious problems shortly thereafter. Further, these young infants chose or preferred to look at one thing and then kept looking at it, and they preferred *non-social* stimuli and remained fixated on such stimuli even when there were other good things to pay attention to (as a typically developing child would). They have more interest in objects than people, a trait that will begin to repeat itself over and over as they develop.

A triad of autism symptoms

Whether you are reading an article about infants, children, adolescents, or adults, many if not most discussions about autism begin the same way. Either they mention Kanner's (1943) paper, which is mainly a collection of case studies, or they discuss the three main criteria that make up the diagnosis of autism. These three main criteria are often drawn from the *Diagnostic and Statistical Manual of Mental Disorders* (DSM-V-TR and now the DSM-V), which originally listed autism as one of the pervasive developmental disorders (PDD). The slightly older version of autism is worth reviewing here, because remember, right now we are interested in how we conceived of this disorder in all the ways it has been defined. Just prior to the DSM-V, autism was defined as a lifelong disorder where the symptoms are present before age 3, and therefore it is usually diagnosed in infancy or early childhood. It was noted to be marked by impairments in a triad of symptoms: 1) social interactions (socialization), 2) communication, and 3) a restricted set of interests or repetitive behaviors. Such broad criteria can, as one would suspect, be expressed in many different ways, so fortunately the earlier DSM provided additional information to assist clinicians. For example, social interaction impairments could affect a wide range of behaviors that change as the child grows up. As an infant or toddler, there may be impairments in eye-gaze, poor understanding of facial expressions, and a lack of shared enjoyment. Young children with autism will not show or bring things to others, engage in joint attention, or initiate/respond to social overtures. They may use others as "tools" in play (including unusual use of another's body or body part), and interact with disinterest, as if no one was even around them. An older child with autism additionally has difficulty with social conventions, empathy, showing insight into his or her emotions, and will not generally seek peer-related, shared enjoyment with others. This child may prefer solitary activities and have little conceptualization of (or concern for) the needs, joys, or distress of others. In essence, the autistic child is alone in a world of others.

The earlier DSM likewise had a number of descriptors about verbal communication. Persons with autism may not be at all able to speak, may have some speech or some form of speech delay, or can have full speech but be basically unable to sustain a reasonable conversation with another person. Delays can take the form of idiosyncratic language, limited gesturing, unusual intonation or rhythm, or even repetitive use of meaningless or "heard" language, such as books, commercials, or songs. In terms of understanding language there is a wide range of abilities, but jokes and humor are particularly difficult for some reason, and communicative play is often out of context or described as "mechanical." Similar to the social impairments, communication impairments are not always simply a delay or absence of language. Instead, these impairments take on a particular form that relates to the curious nature of autism. In other words, when speech is present, it is impaired in relation to *another person*. The person with autism cannot perceive the other person's interest or role in a mutual conversation, and has no interest in learning to create normal speech patterns. Further, beyond not understanding statements or questions, he or she has difficulty with *humor*, which interestingly involves simultaneous (or dual) comprehension of multiple meanings or words or situations. Please note (as this information begins to inform our theory) that similar to socialization symptoms where people are identified as "tools," communication for the person with autism is described as "mechanical." As a group we could begin to conceive of autism as a conceptual absence of other people—and in its place, the person with autism simply sees another "thing."

Finally, the earlier version of the DSM discussed the third set of criteria for an autism diagnosis, restricted and repetitive patterns of behavior. Persons with autism may inflexibly focus on one particular topic with intensity, insist on performing meaningless routines or motor mannerisms, or they may have a persistent preoccupation with "parts of objects." This leg of the autism triad of symptoms can be present in as many forms as the communication symptoms, and is often compared to behaviors associated with obsessive-compulsive disorder (OCD). Persons with autism may line items up, insist on a particular order to various elements in the environment, or repetitively play with the same item or watch the same video clip over and over. Any interruption in these various routines, rituals, or movements can at times lead to intense distress, far beyond what would normally be expected, or some persons with autism have no response at all to interruption of routines. They simply move on to the next item or activity of interest. Interestingly, the earlier DSM noted that there may be a pre-occupation with "parts of objects," a fascination with movement of objects, or an intense attachment to an inanimate object. As with the socialization and communication symptoms, even these clearly identified, standard, and accepted diagnostic criteria suggest some special relationship to the things in the world around the person with autism. Whether the people in this world are "tools," communicative play is "mechanical," or parts of objects are more interesting than the whole thing, there is a pervasive difference between typically developing persons and persons with autism in that everything is a "thing," and for that child there has never been an "other." This may seem unusual or even benign to the reader, but as we shall see, it is the early awareness of and "linking" to another person as a person and not an inanimate object, that allows normal thinking to develop. Again, we see that autism is aptly named in that self, same self, and only a singular self exists.

Recent findings from the DSM-V

The newest version of the manual that describes mental disorders, the DSM-V, somewhat changed this earlier set of descriptors, starting with naming the disorder "autism spectrum disorder" or "ASD." Renaming the disorder allowed clinicians and practitioners the opportunity to see the various symptoms of the disorder on a sort of array; the symptoms could now vary in intensity, as well as particular presentation or combination of presentations. For ASD, the disorder must still develop in the early developmental period and be differentiated from an intellectual disability, and there is the addition of three levels of general severity. But in this current edition, there are two main criteria of symptoms instead of three, the result of combining deficits in social interaction and communication into one. The first criteria, a deficit in social interaction and communication, includes problems in social reciprocity, being generally poor at knowing when to start and stop a conversation, and thinking of things that might be of interest to the other person. It also includes impairments in nonverbal communication, like understanding eye contact or the meaning of a gesture. With these problems at play, it is understandable that an additional deficit in this category includes problems making and keeping friendships, sharing imaginative play, or having an interest in other people.

The second and last criteria involves the restrictive and repetitive patterns of behavior such as repetitive motor movements, repetitive use of objects, inflexibility, and an insistence on sameness, as well as restricted, fixated interests on unusual ideas or objects. Finally, there can also be an unusual response to the sensory aspects of objects or the environment in terms of severity. Again, this new version of autism states that it happens very early in a child's development, and presents itself in a "spectrum" of possibilities. Autism may not be present at birth, but it could be. This reality suggests that both genetic and environmental influences could play a role, or perhaps the effects of environment on the "genetic unfolding" of typical human cognitive and emotional development. If there are severities, then what you are born with, what happens to you, or the effect of what happens to your unfolding of genetics early in life, can be affected to different degrees. The severities might also be reversed or altered to varying degrees as well, depending on the strength of the genetic component vs. the environmental one, or the interplay between the two. Regarding the newly combined and arranged criteria, there remains a real problem with other people: Understanding them, conceiving of them as people and not objects, imagining what the other person wants or needs (or caring about that), and understanding what specific eye movements or gestures mean or indicate. There continues to be a mechanical, repetitive, object focus in the newly defined ASD, and a desire to keep things the same. Finally, for persons with autism, there is sometimes a high or low sensitivity to one's surroundings. This means that a person with this disorder might be excessively sensitive to what a typically developing person finds innocuous, such as overhead lighting, multiple conversations taking place in the same room, or patterns in flooring or wall paper. Conversely, persons with autism may enjoy getting blood drawn, the taste of excessively spicy foods, or hitting his or her head on hard surfaces, which the typically developing person would generally find unpleasant.

Associated symptoms provide important clues

While we can begin to get an idea of what autism is by examining both the earlier and most recent criteria, it is the associated symptoms that provide important clues as to the nature of autism. These associated symptoms don't seem to fit nicely into the standard autism triad. One example is impaired "awareness," which is typically associated with socialization. However, this symptom extends beyond just how one person interacts with another, and seems to suggest that persons with autism may or may not even know that others in the environment exist. When a person with autism is in a group of people, how does he or she perceive those other people? Are they perceived as moveable, animated objects? If so, how does this explain why some children with autism express pleasure at seeing their parent? Another example of an associated symptom, which is present in the newer diagnostic version's social communication domain, is "limited make-believe play." From a diagnostic perspective, this symptom was originally wedged between idiosyncratic language and abnormal speech intonation, whereas now it is actually "sharing of imaginative play" not a deficit in imaginative play. What does make-believe or imagination-based play have to do with communication and speech development? It's as if the creators of this diagnostic category felt determined to make them fit one way or another, a difficult task indeed. The fact is that they do not go together easily in the categories identified, mainly because we have a very limited understanding of what autism is and where it comes from, so the categories themselves are most likely misleading. Because practitioners are unable to draw upon a coherent theory that encompasses the myriad categories and factors that make up a diagnostic framework, we are left to our own devices as to how to best capture the many complex and curious signs of autism.

More associated symptoms of autism add to our already bizarre listing of criteria include uneven cognitive skills; various behavioral challenges such as impulsive aggression or tantrums; "scripting" or repetitive self-talk; painfully flat affect or emotionality; and abnormalities of mood are all commonly present. In addition, a person with autism may not fear things they should fear, or may be excessively fearful about things that are innocuous. They may have unusual eating or sleeping habits, and it is not uncommon to display self-injurious behavior (SIB). These behaviors can take many forms, including finger-or wrist-biting, head-hitting, eye-poking, and many others. This grouping of behavioral symptoms includes some of the most difficult to understand and disturbing features of autism, and they are often difficult to stop or at least reduce. One of the more effective approaches to addressing SIB (as well as many other behavioral challenges) is to determine the true reason for, or function of, the behavior, a process known as functional behavioral analysis (FBA). A popular outcome of FBA is the finding that the function is not to obtain something or avoid something, but rather it is purely "sensory" or "automatic." This means that the person with autism is simply seeking out or *enjoying* the sensory stimulation associated with this behavior. In addition to the other symptoms listed, how do we integrate the apparent enjoyment of self-induced pain or mutilation? What's more, because it is neither socialization nor communication (usually), is it appropriate to consider this a repetitive behavior? While it certainly is repetitive, SIB seems conceptually different from lining up pencils or watching a video repeatedly. As perplexing and frustrating as this all is to understand, this symptom gives us another clue into the origins of autism and is one of the many symptoms that a comprehensive theory of autism needs to be able to accommodate.

A number of researchers have added even further to the list of features associated with a diagnosis of autism, which is helpful as we look for a way to conceive of the origins of autism or ASD. For example, Courchesne et al. (1990) note that children with autism do not imitate others, and typically do not take turns or share attention with others. They prefer solitary play and may appear disinterested in the behaviors and actions of others. In the communication domain, these researchers suggest that some additional features include echolalic speech (repeating back the last thing that one hears), and the unusual presence of pronoun reversal. In pronoun reversal, "you" is often or always stated instead of "I," which is another seemingly bizarre and unrelated symptom that is another hint as to the nature of autism. In a related vein, persons with autism often apply a concrete, literal interpretation of phrases and metaphors. For example, if you said something like "we will put that idea in our back pocket," that is exactly where the person with autism would look—in your back pocket. Interestingly, much like some forms of humor, metaphors such as these again require simultaneous comprehension of two meanings, the literal one and the conceptual one. Children with autism also don't typically search for things. If something has consistently been in the same place, he or she is able to find it there, but if you told this person that thing was "hidden in the house," he or she would typically just stop and shut down. When one begins to think more along these abstract lines in considering the nature of autism, it almost begins to make sense in a curious and vague sort of way.

Returning for a moment to pronoun reversal, this symptom has received a notable amount of research in past years, and is a good example of the heterogeneity of the disorder. Hobson and his colleagues (Hobson, Lee and Hobson, 2010) reviewed research that suggests highly varied presentations of pronoun reversal in terms of frequency. One research article reported 17 out of 25 (nearly 70%) children with autism display this feature, while in other articles show a mere 12% of participants reversed pronouns. This wide span of results is commonly found in autism research, again reflecting the heterogeneity of the autism diagnosis and helping to fuel the shift in thinking of autism as a spectrum disorder. It's important to emphasize again that there are always exceptions with autism. For everything discussed in this section, there will be someone who says, "Wait. My child with autism is able to do that!" This is common and part of the curious nature of the disorder. As we have noted, an autism diagnosis can include high or low intelligence, speech or no speech, challenging behaviors or no challenging behaviors, paying some attention to others or none, and the list goes on. While there is no actual ASD diagnostic category but only indicators of severity, the people that a researcher selects as his or her participants can vary widely and the product will still be considered research on persons diagnosed with autism. The diagnostic criteria are simply so broad that the variety of diagnostic triad combinations are seemingly endless. This of course can affect the results of any given research study, and unfortunately, while persons with more severe presentations of the disorder might be considered the neediest, persons with less pronounced or severe presentations are often those included in research for obvious reasons.

What we know so far

To summarize what we know so far, there are unusual and highly varied symptoms of autism present in infancy, minimally coherent and homogenous diagnostic features for ASD in children, adolescents, and adults, and further associated features that only add to the complexity of this disorder. Research is typically based on highly varied sets of participants leading often to findings that only reflect the wide array of presentations of ASD. To complicate the picture further, different features of autism are present at different ages and then change across the lifespan. You might have a sense that these symptoms do go together is some way, although right now it is difficult to figure out exactly how. But there seems to be a theme of sorts, a central idea that we can't as yet put our finger on. At this point perhaps, all we can say is that there may be something central here about how other people are understood or perceived, and there is confusion about how they are different from inanimate objects in the environment. We can say with some certainty that there is some sort of early disinterest in people and a preference for inanimate objects that must be linked to an expanding network of associated symptoms. But that framework seems like a tangled web of unrelated or at best, loosely related symptoms. What is happening early in life that might lead to something as complex as autism? How does autism come about and is it present at birth? And how could something as basic as impaired early eye gaze result in a disorder that includes symptoms as obscure as not being able to understand a joke? These are difficult questions, but it seems clear that practitioners and parents alike would benefit from a coherent and encompassing theory of autism, one that ties together most of the core and associated symptoms and explains why it happens early and with varying presentations, as well as a theory that accounts for both early and later symptoms. Once you realize that early identification with person (and not object) results in the ability to *think about*, symbolize, imagine, or represent one thing with something else, all of what I have just reviewed makes perfect sense.

Chapter 2: What We Know About Genes, Environment, and Treatment

The pathogenesis of autism is largely unknown (Bodfish, 2004), but we do know a little about prevalence, and the role of both genetics and environment. Unfortunately, what we know does not make much sense to researchers as yet. It will probably come as no surprise that the number of documented cases of autism has been increasing steadily over the past 20 years—and it's not clear whether this increase is the result of more actual cases of autism or simply better/more inclusive identification and diagnosis. When I tell people that I work with children with autism, this is probably the most common area they ask about, and I think they are surprised that I can't really give them the kind of answer they are looking for. People seem to know not only that this disorder is increasing, but that for many years, research has been targeted at trying to find the source of the increase. In 1994 the rate of children diagnosed with autism was approximately 3.5 out of 10,000, or .00035% (APA, 2000), but by 2009, the rate had risen to an estimated 1% of children ages 3 to 17 (Kogan et al., 2009)—and no one knows for sure why this is happening. This rate rose steadily in reports from the CDC in 2012 through 2016, and by 2018, the prevalence of autism reported by the CDC rose to 1 in 68 children, or 0.015%. A recent article suggested even higher rates of prevalence (Kogan et al., 2018) at 1 child in 40.

While we don't know the exact cause of this increase, fortunately there are some things about the disorder that we do know. For example, rates of autism were higher among low-income families and children born pre-term; what's more, children born in the United States were more likely to be diagnosed with autism than foreign-born children in the study by Kogan et al. We also know that males are likely to be diagnosed with autism three to four times more than females, which suggests a genetic origin. Further support for a genetic link comes from the fact that research on the risk of recurrence in a (genetically similar) sibling ranges between 3% and 8% (Szatmari et al., 1998). However, concordance rates in genetically identical twins (monozygotic siblings) are less than 100% (Santangelo and Tsatsanis, 2006), which supports the idea that environmental factors may also play a role. But despite a desperate, extensive, and very expensive search, there is no known single biological marker or gene that is responsible for the expression of autism. There are some genetic commonalities that researchers have found in a small percentage of children with autism, but no genetics common to all. Although autism can be detected at a very young age, unlike Down Syndrome or Fragile X Syndrome, it is clearly the result of both a combination of genetic *and* environmental factors, which dramatically complicates our understanding. Which genes contribute to the emergence of autism, and how? What environmental factors play a role? And how do these two components combine so early in life to result in such a pervasive and debilitating disorder?

What we can learn by studying twins

Before we move on to discuss other research on genetics, it is important to note that the Szatmari et al. (1998) article discusses a lot about the genetics of autism, mainly by summarizing twin studies. Because there are not a lot of twins with autism, the few studies with this population are considered important and key in trying to understand this disorder. These studies however, make a complex situation even more complex. In Szatmari's summary tables, the reader will find information on monozygotic twins and dyzigotic (fraternal) twins, who have respectively, 100% and 50% (on average by descent, as with siblings) identical genetic material.

23

There are four such studies listed, and the concordance rates for monozygotic twins ranges from 36% to 95%, with an average of 73%. This means that on average, if you have the exact same genetic material, you have a 3 out of 4 chance of developing autism. In these same studies, the concordance rates for dyzigotic twins are also listed, and with an average of 50% of the same genetic material by descent, one would expect concordance rates in the 20% to 50% range. However, what are actually listed are extremely *low* concordance rates in these types of twins: 0% in three of the four studies listed and 23% in the last study. Out of a total of 48 pairs of dyzigotic twins, only four found both children developing autism. As one would expect, this is about the same overall concordance percentage (8%) as non-twin siblings when you average all the research findings—and the one study that found the highest concordance rate at 23% is the one that has been criticized due to nonsystematic sampling. All of the other studies showed 0% concordance rates. This complicated picture may suggest that autism is a "whole person" disorder, meaning that the roots of autism are found in a process that draws from not one, but from many of the complex and pervasive sources of our human experience. This finding is another piece of the puzzle that we will put in our back pocket, which seems to be filling with a number of interesting clues as to the origins of autism.

Where genetics, environment, and psychology intersect

Santangelo and Tsatsanis (2006) carefully stated, "It is expected that several genes are involved that, in combination, give rise to an increased vulnerability to autism" (p.77). Researchers have found perhaps 10 to 15 (or more) genetic areas that may play key roles (the 15q11-q13 region has been found to be the most common location of chromosomal abnormalities in persons with autism), but it is disheartening to realize that even positive findings of genetic commonalities only account for about 8% to 15% of persons diagnosed with the disorder. One way to hypothesize a stronger role of genes is to use terms like the ones noted in the quote above: "in combination" and "vulnerability." Such terms suggest that we have been too limited in our single-gene, single-region, or absolute "gene X = autism" search; perhaps we need to extend our search to multiple *combinations*. Or, perhaps there are complex combinations of genes that make us *vulnerable* to an even wider variety of environmental factors. At this point, we've now moved into what we know about many psychological disorders. For example, couldn't we say the same thing about schizophrenia or depression? Although these conditions often emerge at certain ages and can run in families, aren't disorders such as these likely to result from complex combinations of genetic codes that open the door to an array of environmental influences that result in the disorder? The answer to this is a resounding Yes in that there are genetic similarities in persons with these disorders, yet not everyone with these similar codes develops the disorders listed.

But the *early* emergence of autism as compared to other psychological disorders does pose a special challenge because there is far less time for environment to play its supposed role. One way of addressing this challenge is to suggest that the source of "environmental influence" is not an event or experience, but rather a "toxin" that exploits a genetic mutation early in life and/or causes some of the known abnormal brain development (e.g., Bauman and Kemper, 2003). For example, at the 2008 International Meeting for Autism Research (IMFAR), Brenda Eskenazi and Eric Roberts reported on a longitudinal study called "CHAMACOS." In this study, these researchers found that a mutation of a gene responsible for detoxification of pesticides may have contributed to the emergence of pervasive developmental disorders (PDD), a group of disorders characterized by delays in the development of socialization and communication skills. Not all of the children exposed to pesticides developed PDD, but the ones who did were genetically vulnerable. Beyond toxins such as pesticides, other environmental substances such as heavy metals, infections, and air pollution have been suggested to contribute to the "chronic pathophysiology of neuroinflammation and oxidative stress" (Herbert, 2005) of autism, yet not one of them has been scientifically proven to be causal for autism.

In essence, we are left with a conclusion that most would consider a bit obvious and of little practical value in trying to understand autism: Beyond the fact that more males develop the disorder than females, and concordance rates are higher in monozygotic than dizygotic twins, all we know about genetics and autism is that there are a few regions of common genetic anomalies present in about 8% to 15% of the autism population. These anomalies may or may not create a vague vulnerability to any number of environmental substances or influences, but none have been scientifically found to actually be consistently causal. As Szatmari et al. (1998) noted when they considered autism similar in etiology to schizophrenia or bipolar disorder, "No evidence for Mendelian subforms exist and each genetic locus appears to provide only a relatively small proportion of the increased risk to the disorder" (p.365). Not only does all this tell us very little about where autism comes from (except that genetic risk may come from just about anywhere in our DNA), but it does not explain how autism developed for all the children without the genetic anomalies.

If both the genetic and environmental toxin approaches leave us wanting in terms of a satisfactory explanation as to the origins of autism, are there psychological theories? Yes, and these include a variety of ideas including Baron-Cohen's Theory of Mind (ToM) deficit theory, Norman and Shallice's executive function theory, and Frith's central coherence theory. A full discussion of each theory is beyond the scope of this book, but the concepts are basically that autism derives from an inability to understand the thinking and perspectives of others; it stems from an impairment in early development of the main cognitive processes, or a limited ability to understand context or see the "big picture," respectively. Each has impressive attributes or ideas, but each also leaves the reader wanting something more. If we are to turn to a psychological theory of pathogenesis, how do these theories account for autism being diagnosable around age 2? Could a complex and varying combination of genetic and environmental factors be affecting and altering in degrees early psychological/developmental/cognitive processes? This certainly seems to be a possibility and aligns most closely with Baron-Cohen's ToM perspective and the theory we will propose later in this book.

Effective treatment of autism in early childhood

Perhaps exploring why certain types of interventions are effective in treating autism might be more illuminating than searching for genetic or environmental causes. There have been volumes written on this topic, but because we know autism is expressed early in infancy and it is only during infancy that intense treatment can sometimes affect core symptoms (and not only associated symptoms), we will focus here on interventions employed during early childhood. Specifically, while many techniques have been shown to affect established symptoms of autism in later childhood, adolescence, and even adulthood (i.e., exchange/communication systems, medications, social scripts, daily schedule systems, functional behavior analysis, applied behavior analysis procedures, etc.), it is only during infancy that distinct alterations can perhaps be made in foundational areas and indicators such as cognitive development and educational placement. One of the first research studies that showed significant core improvements was conducted by Lovaas (1987). This researcher worked with 19 children with autism who were approximately 3.5 years of age or under, and he exposed them to 2 years or more of treatment that averaged 40 hours per week. It was reported that nearly 90% of the children in the experimental group achieved significant intellectual and educational gains—and these gains were maintained years later. Despite some methodological flaws and an inability (so far) for other researchers to fully replicate these enormous gains, versions of the interventions used by Lovaas, which were all based on the principles of applied behavior analysis (ABA), continue today to be the preferred method of intervention for children with autism. This is due to generally supportive follow-up research (e.g., Frea & McNervey, 2008).

So, what actually happened during treatment in the Lovaas study, and what types of ABA interventions are used today? Early treatment models used a "discrete trial" methodology, along with ignoring, removing reinforcement for, or punishing (with a moderate slap on the thigh) non-desired behaviors (this punishment is not generally considered appropriate or necessary today). For the discrete trial goals, a specific behavioral target was identified and modified by gaining the child's attention, giving a discrete instruction, and then reinforcing the correct response or providing any number of correction procedures for non-correct responses. This process was repeated in massed trials, and then when a measured behavioral goal was attained, a new one was put in place. Behavioral targets were individualized based on that child's particular needs and functioning levels, and targets could include anything from imitation skills, to receptive and expressive language skills, to pre-academic or daily living skills. Such "drills" of skill sets typically became more and more complex, and previously learned behaviors were reviewed periodically so no skill gains were lost. Treatment today often continues to employ variations of this discrete trial approach with explicit teaching of additional skills such as joint attention, taking turns, or interactive play—with sessions administered by both clinicians and parents throughout the day. However, there are a number of additional therapeutic elements that have also been found to be key in effecting a change.

Associated ABA techniques and now more naturally occurring and interpersonal components are commonly added to augment discrete trial teaching. For example, token systems can be used to reinforce desired behaviors, and functional behavior analysis can be used to help minimize inappropriate behaviors. Incidental teaching reinforces skills and behaviors outside of the discrete trial dyad, and parents take part in specialized training so that intervention can take place throughout the day. Various other ABA-derived techniques are integrated into programs, such as visual schedules that provide a clear plan as to what is happening next, picture exchange communication systems that allow expression of wants and needs in the absence of speech, or predictable routines and environmental structure. Rogers and Vismara (2008) note many of these interventions as components of treatment models described as "probably efficacious." The popular versions of these models are Pivotal Response Treatment (PRT) and the Early Start Denver Model (ESDM), which elaborate on one element of treatment or another. PRT for example, uses a combined developmental and ABA perspective to increase a child's desire to learn skills related to imitation, language, and play. For the PRT therapist, the "pivotal" areas are those that when targeted, improve other related areas that were not necessarily targeted. Examples of pivotal areas include motivation, responsiveness to cue, empathy, and others (Koegel & Koegel, 2006). So, to improve early labeling and requesting, the PRT therapist might affect motivation by creating obstacle situations that serve to elicit communication attempts, and at the same time modeling appropriate prompts for the infant. Similarly, the ESDM employs selected teaching techniques within the framework of an interpersonal relationship. But it is the *one-on-one engagement and human interaction* that is often the main focus, and the scientific and systematic data-based decision-making that form the unique centerpieces of many of these effective forms of treatment.

For a child starting treatment, a main focus is usually on the basic behaviors noted above that are oftentimes missing or minimal for the child with autism. For example, attending to social stimuli such as responding to one's name being called, orienting to attempts by others to engage in joint attention, and basic imitation are common places to start. While these behaviors can be addressed in a discrete trial format and often are, it is the incidental teaching with interpersonal stimuli and cues in more naturalistic settings that allows skills to be generalized. Further, combining naturalistic and play-based teaching strategies in addition to discrete trial teaching makes skill acquisition more likely to become part of the child's spontaneous, functional communication. But regardless of the discrete trial or play-focused format, what is always happening in these interactions? One key feature is obvious, yet it must be clearly identified for our purposes: All of the most effective forms of intervention require interaction with another person, whether it is a teacher, parent, or clinician. These interventions can't be administered effectively in any other way, and there is no current form of effective treatment for autism that does not involve someone else being present, gaining the child's attention, establishing eye-contact, and then baiting the environment, providing reinforcement, or correcting a behavioral response in a rapid, planned, and repeated manner. The learning theory portion of this treatment equation should not come as a surprise because interventions based on these principles have been proven effective for the past 60 years. It is the human contact element that is essential—no video, no self-management, no toys, no Skinnerian reinforcement machine, and no set of physical surroundings will do the trick. And it is not simply that there is a person present, but the nature and duration of that person's presence seems to make the difference between effective and non-effective treatment. While the 40 hours used by Lovaas may no longer be the essential number, 15 to 25 hours of intensive professional treatment, accompanied by trained parent engagement at other times, is currently the standard.

More recently there has been more and more focus on the natural, interpersonal interactions and the intersection of they have with a wide array of positive ABA components and practices. To this point Schreibman et al. (2015) recently discussed attributes of effective intervention approaches, and described these as "naturalistic developmental behavioral interventions" (NDBIs). The core components of NDBIs includes interventions that cross cognitive, social, language, and play developmental domains and focus on pivotal skill areas, and interventions that are delivered in naturalistic, emotionally meaningful and socially interactive contexts. Additionally, NDBIs use known behavioral strategies that build on established skills and routines. In this description, the behavioral components almost seem to be a given, and what has become more apparent as time goes on is the importance of not focusing on singular skills, but developmental domains; not focusing on part of the person, but rather the whole person as a developing being; not focusing on tasks, but on emotions and social contexts. In essence, researchers seem to be finding that the behavioral approach is helpful and an essential component, but what may be more essential for real gains to be made and changes to occur has something to do with people, feelings, and the social connections made early in life.

So, what have we learned?

In summary, while there is clearly a heritable component to autism, genetics alone do not tell the whole story and any

31

genetically significant areas are likely spread across vast amounts of genetic material. Our best explanation at this point in time is that there may be a small subset of children with autism who have any one of a number of chromosomal anomalies, and these anomalies may have put these children at risk under certain environmental conditions. But because there is a vast majority of children with autism who *do not* carry these genetic anomalies, we must conclude that: 1) We simply have not yet found the responsible genetic marker, 2) There are environmental substances or influences at play in the creation of autism not yet identified, and/or 3) Beyond the 8% to 15% of children with known genetic anomalies, there are a variety of "soft" predispositions to developing autism that are not clearly identifiable in one's genetic make-up. What I am suggesting by this last item is that there remains the possibility that there may be a typical temperament, set of traits, type of general approach to the world, or type of "being" that is a result of and caused by many bits of the whole of our genetic endowment—this is not a new idea, but one we will return to later.

All infants have certain temperaments, and we will note that such combinations of qualities are not evidenced in any specific genetic pattern or region. For example, any given infant might be generally irritable, passive, happy, or agreeable, yet you won't find a set of genetic markers where these qualities came from. With autism, what would such a temperament be and how could it interact with the environment so early in life to cause such pervasive effects and impairments? While it seems obvious in retrospect, looking for a gene or responsible set of genes for autism presumes that this disorder is a singular, coherent "thing" that unfolds like eye color—and clearly, it is not. If only it were so simple! Similarly, there is no single known substance or environmental influence that causes autism, which suggests that it is also not solely an environmentally induced problem. It is more likely to be something in the middle, something partially genetic and partially environmental, though it must be something pervasive across the genetic code and a quality that is present and active very early in development. It is interesting to note that for an infant who spends 20 to 40 hours per week being encouraged to pay attention to another person in a planned and intensive manner, the very core symptoms or foundational cognitive skills can be affected. In certain cases, this type of intensive, planned, human engagement has even been reported to lead to cases of "recovery."

Before we move on to what typical early development looks like, let's take a moment to recap what we have learned so far:

1) Autism spectrum disorder (ASD) is either present from birth or emerges very early in a child's development; it varies in its severity, and it changes as the person matures or develops in certain ways.

2) Infants/toddlers and young children with ASD can have a wide set of highly varied presentations, but the core criteria include problems with social interaction and communication, and a preference for rigidity, repetition and sameness.

3) There are some other symptoms sometimes present that don't fit particularly well with those in #2 above, such as pronoun reversal, lack of humor and searching behavior, a focus on parts of objects, absence of embarrassment, a generally "mechanical" approach to the world, and unusual behaviors such as self-injury.

4) There seems to be a general and unique problem represented by the symptom of impaired social interactions and communication: Specifically, the person with ASD can't generally imagine the thoughts or feelings of another person well. He or she can't imagine what a subtle eye

33

movement might mean, or a slight move of the head. He or she can't generate or take part in the process of imaginary play, or having one thing represent another (in often social routines). He or she can't imagine what a saying means, and interprets these statements very literally.

5) ASD is not a purely genetic or environmental disorder; it is more likely something in the middle. There may be a genetically predisposed temperament that, depending on the strength of this temperament and the presence of early environmental factors, sets the stage for affecting early psychological development.

6) There are only a few treatments that help or work on this problem, but they work to the extent that they have good behavioral components and also bring the toddler or child's focus back to people, and encourage a cross domain cognitive-developmental progress to occur. They require a person to be effective, whether that person is working on imitation, language, play, turn-taking, or any other number of skills. The essential component is the person.

Chapter 3: Typical Early Development and the Emergence of Imagination

What I have summarized in Chapter 2 provides enough information to begin thinking about what a reasonable and logical theory of autism might include. One possibility is that in the majority of cases, autism results from genetically "softer" infantile traits, preferences, or ways of being that collide with an important early developmental process and/or environmental element, causing the infant to veer off of some aspect of the typical developmental trajectory. Although many aspects of the young child are developing in the first year of life, I will suggest that it is the *very process of thinking* that is affected which, as I will show, accounts for nearly all of the symptoms of autism. This is by no means a new idea, but how it happens and what is actually happening have not been clearly identified in a manner that does all the things a comprehensive or useful theory needs to do. Of course, no infant comes into the world with adult thinking capabilities; these form over time and are a function of a developmental sequence that takes place in the context of a (hopefully) active, engaging, and appropriately stimulating environment. We know that without this stimulation, devastating damage is likely; one only needs to look at infants deprived of early human care, attention, and interaction (such as those in third-world orphanages) to see this. Although "thinking" is a broad term, since we know that autism emerges by the second year, it follows that we must look at which aspects of thinking are forming just before and during this early period. To do this, we need to know what is happening with typically developing infants with regard to their ability to think in both their first and second years of life. It turns out that this is a particularly interesting time of development.

In the following section, I would like to acknowledge Jennifer Van Reet who authored much of the corresponding information in our 2011 article. While we know that newborns clearly can't and don't think like adults, it is difficult to conceive of what the mental world of a newborn might be like. Years ago, a child was considered a "tabula rasa" or blank slate, ready and waiting to be filled with information from the outside world. But a child does not come into the world without any thinking abilities; quite the contrary. Research has shown that even a fetus in the third trimester can become accustomed or "habituate" to a sound (Kisilevsky et al., 1999), and newborns can recognize sounds experienced in utero (DeCasper and Spence, 1986). These facts suggest that even before birth, the fetus or newborn has the capability to somehow "know" something—even if this "knowing" is usually a primitive form of simple recognition. Being able to "recognize" is often considered one of the most basic behaviors that signifies thinking because it suggests that some type of memory or "primary representation" has been created. While this is an impressive feat, the ability to recognize is still rather unsophisticated when we compare it to the wide range of adult thinking abilities that commonly emerge.

Within 6 months of birth, the infant has typically made some impressive cognitive strides. Research has shown that by 3 months, he or she knows something about gravity (Baillergeon et al., 1992), and soon after that, there is evidence of infants recognizing simple goal-directed behavior (Woodward, 1998). While the infant clearly cannot explicitly manipulate ideas about gravity or understand actual intention, these studies do indicate precursor abilities: The infant "recognizes" that heavy objects don't usually hang in the air, and hands can be reaching for a *certain* toy. By 8 months, the typically developing infant can demonstrate "object permanence," meaning that they know an object continues to exist even if it is hidden from view (Willatts,

1984). This skill is significant, as it indicates that the infant has developed a primitive version of a skill to which we will devote much time and attention—imagination. For an infant to search for a hidden object, they must have moved slightly beyond recognition of people, objects, or patterns in a cognitive sense. In other words, they can't just be cognitively experiencing the world as an ever-present "now." Looking for something unseen suggests that the developing infant can now actually conceive of the item in a mental way. He or she is now able to "imagine" its existence and location, and hold that mental conceptualization while searching. Note that we will use the term "imagination" in its broadest sense, defined as any behavioral evidence of a generated mental image, representative symbol, or concept. We are not using this term as it is typically employed, as a component of creativity or the formation of new ideas.

The "9-month revolution" in cognitive development

When researchers are discussing these various mental abilities, typically they use the term "primary representation" when considering recognition, and "meta-representation" when more sophisticated, imagination-based abilities are evident. We will return to these concepts later, but it is notable that shortly after object permanence surfaces, a range of social skills typically emerge prior to the first birthday. These skills are so incredible and denote such a cognitive leap that they have often been called the "9-month revolution" (Tomasello, 1999). It is at this time that we typically begin to see many of these social skills, the lack of which we will see, signifies autism. Specifically, infants begin to attend to and enjoy more the emotional expressions of other people for important information. The "emotional stance" of other people is "taken on" by the infant (Woodard and Van Reet, 2011), and behaviors such as joint attention, increasingly deferred imitation, and pointing suddenly emerge. Shared interest in an item or event suggests that something important has happened from a cognitive perspective, and a whole world has opened up for the developing infant. This skill is the key component to our theory of what autism is, but one needs to understand that this skill is not necessarily a given. It comes from somewhere in a genetic sense, is influenced by factors in the environment, and may emerge, may not emerge, or may only partially emerge. Much like sexuality, there are both genetic components and events that happen early in life that affect one's preferences and behavior, and these are complex and unique to each individual.

Woodard and Van Reet proposed (as have others previously) that this shift in thinking abilities demonstrates that the infant has apparently gained an early version of "thinking about": The ability to "utilize an alternative perspective. They can interpret and identify with what another person is feeling, looking at, and pointing to…" (p.216). This incredible shift in skills and abilities has been the focus of much research because it marks that emergence of a level of thinking far beyond object permanence; now there is not only a real object and perception of the object, but a real *person* and perception of the *mental state* of that person relative to the shared perception of object! This development clearly is a significant "step up" on the ladder of cognitive abstraction and is imagination itself. When discussing this shift with colleagues and parents of typically developing children, not one has denied these events occurring. This shift has been referred to as entrance into the human, social world of existence, although one needs to be careful not to infer that this means someone with autism is "less human." This early ability to *think about* relative to other people is an avenue to one aspect of being, yet one so central that an impairment has been deemed a disorder.

A working hypothesis of autism

Our central hypothesis (so far) is this: Autism is the result

39

of impairment in the cognitive step known as the 9-month revolution in thinking, which allows the ability to *think about* or experience a thing, as well as mentally or otherwise represent that thing, and all the associated skills that flow from it as a person develops over a lifetime. Note that these things again, can be on a continuum or spectrum: It is one thing to know that a box of corn flakes continues to exist even if I can't see it in the cabinet. It is quite another thing to presume the mental state of another person by watching their eyes and facial expression, and then take this one step further and conceive of that mental state. These two abilities are related in that clearly the first lends itself to the complexity of the next, which is consistent with the "cascading" effects of these early development events noted in our hypothesis. Also, note for future reference that the object comes first in the process of thinking development for the infant, followed by person and mental state of the person.

Typical development of the 9-month revolution in thinking allows an infant to share in the emotional states and internal experiences of others, creating the possibility for many new social interchanges. Early on, this development opens the door to many early behaviors. Infants begin to point out people and objects of interest to others, rather than simply allowing others to take the lead. Because the infant can conceive of your thinking, now an attempt is made to direct your attention as he or she seeks to join in emotional exchanges during typical development, and become what Van Reet calls a true "social partner." Since there is recognition by the child that you are able to think too, social engagement becomes purposeful. As time goes on during the second year of development, children build upon these new-found abilities and become able to imagine mental states that differ from their own. By 18 months they can imagine another person's desires (Repacholi and Gopnik, 1997), and actually act on these perceived, alternate mental states. This is the foundation for later discussion of topics that are of interest to the other person—and another skill painfully absent in persons with autism. It is also during this period that we see the behavior that has been the focus of many research studies on autism: pretend play and interactive pretend play. This skill is usually deeply impaired or absent (but not always!) in children with autism because not only does one need to imagine something representing another thing (like a miniature firetruck is a firetruck), but then the child needs to be able to imagine (and be interested in) another person imagining the same thing! In some children and even young adults with autism, the "spectrum" aspect is especially apparent in this aspect of the disorder: You might see a child "fly" a miniature plane, but once you attempt to engage in that activity, the child typically shuns your involvement.

As with our primary and meta-representational concepts, we will return to pretend play later. First, we need to discuss the ways that theorists have explained how this 9-month revolution in thinking takes place. Because it corresponds to when we see the first signs of autism, it is essential to describe what is known (or at least theorized) about this important period of development. It is also important because imagination has cascading benefits as time goes on—empathy, language, humor, and concept of self, to name a few. Try to see if you can conceive of the early symptoms of autism as having an origin in this particular skill of *thinking about*. Once you are able to see the symptoms this way, it makes sense theoretically that these correspond in many ways to the cascading deficits that emerge in the child with autism over time. What we can take from this understanding is that a useful and encompassing theory of autism needs to account for a combined role of genetically pervasive influence and very early environmental factors, and a preponderance of males with the disorder. A theory of autism must explain why the only effective, empirically validated interventions involve many hours of intense contact with people, and focus on processes active in the first year of development. Specifically, the same seemingly effortless changes in thinking for the typical child around the first birthday are absent in the child with autism.

Explanations of the 9-month revolution in thinking—the emergence of imagination

The period of development dubbed the "9-month revolution" clearly bears special importance when we are considering the origins of autism for a number of reasons. First, as noted above, it signifies a monumental change in how the infant behaves and thinks, and these changes directly correspond to the pervasive, resultant abilities that comprise the basic diagnostic indicators for autism. I have suggested that they also correspond to the "cascading" problems commonly seen as autism progresses, meaning that initial delays in infant response or joint attention may not seem so worrisome. Despite being diagnostic indicators, such variations are normal and parents are often told to simply "wait and see." However, these types of behaviors relate directly not only to autism, but many adult thinking abilities and foundational concepts (such as "self") may derive from successful navigation of developmental processes during this period, and thus may be subsequently affected. But focusing on this developmental event explains a lot about autism: I am suggesting first that **autism is the result of early impairment in the development of foundational, early imagination or meta-representational abilities that is the 9-month revolution in thinking, which has cascading effects as the child continues to develop**. This hypothesis explains many symptoms of early and later autism, as well as that the 9-month revolution happens very early in development, making the timing match when the first signs of autism are present. It also shows how the infant typically moves into and through this period of development so seamlessly that there is general agreement that it has a genetic base even though research suggests that a child's development certainly can be affected during this period by environmental influences such as deprivation, toxins, or non-stimulation. So, the combined genetic/environmental roots of autism fit as well. In the next section, we will discuss theorists who have made significant contributions to our knowledge about the 9-month revolution, and consider each of their unique perspectives in turn. We will explore this area because understanding the mechanisms that allow for early imaginative or meta-representational thinking will be central to developing effective interventions.

Jean Piaget

Jean Piaget was one of the great developmental theorists of our time, and one of the first to suggest that early behaviors (such as pretend play) contribute to how we think as adults. Piaget's theories were derived from close observation of children, and based on the idea that reality was constructed from incoming information drawn from the infant's continual engagement with objects and people in his environment. Piaget's developmental perspective of ever-increasing ideas and understanding depended on a core set of central concepts: schemas, assimilation, and accommodation. Schemas are sets of perceptions or ideas that are logically associated with each other; assimilation denotes the addition of information into an existing schema; and accommodation means that a schema itself needs to be adjusted to manage newly assimilated information. While these definitions appear simple, his use and application of these ideas to the various stages of child development that he hypothesized become increasingly complex. Piaget's theories cover a great deal of child development, but we are mainly interested in what he identified as the later section of the "sensori-motor" stage since it corresponds to the latter half of an infant's first year. During this period, the infant moves from simple reflexes to "primary" and then "secondary circular reactions," where awareness of external objects increases and attempts are made to actually reproduce events (such as shaking a rattle rather than just holding or handling it). Further, as the infant repeatedly observes that actions lead to consistent consequences, he or she begins to combine behavior in new ways to accomplish goals, and becomes increasingly flexible and creative in behaviors. At this stage of development, the infant is able to replace trial and error behavior with behavior that he or she *knows* will bring about certain results (Piaget, 1952).

What did Piaget mean by "knowing"—and is it something that happens suddenly and without cause or reason, or is there a progression that leads to this ability? Piaget created an important work that speaks to these questions entitled "Play, Dreams, and Imitation in Childhood" (Piaget, 1962). Interestingly, as with all of Piaget's cited works, this book is of course a translation from French, and originally called "La Formation du Symbol," or "The Formation of the Symbol." In this book, Piaget focuses on the importance of the infant's early imitation abilities, and how they change to support later symbolic, mental representation. He differentiates clearly between very early imitation that is in the presence of a model, and later types of representative imitation, that can be deferred or where something can "stand for" something else. In the more primitive form of imitation, the visual and auditory perceptions in *immediate* experience allow for *immediate* imitation. In time however, the perceptions somehow become available internally, and the infant is able to support the more sophisticated, representative forms of imitation:

"It is imitation that has been interiorized as a draft for future exterior imitation, and marks the junction-point between the sensory-motor and the representative." (p.279)

How or why this "interiorizing" takes place is not nearly as clearly explained as what takes place, but continued assimilation of information via object manipulation is noted to be essential for the emergence of more sophisticated forms of mental representation. A continued influx of sensory perceptions and explorations of the world may create a sort of framework or priming effect (this can only be presumed, as no actual mechanism is proposed by Piaget) for subsequent "symbolic or imaged representation."

With this type of higher representation now active, experimentation can now take place internally rather that externally, and mental planning and prediction become possible. In Piaget's words:

> "It is therefore due to representation that 'mental experience' succeeds actual experimentation and that assimilatory activity can be pursued and purified on a new plane, separate from that of immediate perception or action so properly called." (p.351)

This mental representation ability that emerges allows for a number of other, dependent skills to develop: invention, symbolization, and deferred imitation. These skills all have special significance when we return to our discussion of autism, because a very different thinking component or ability is essential to support them. "Invention" is the ability to spontaneously reorganize (accommodate) information in a rapid manner—to come up with new ways of thinking quickly and efficiently. "Symbolization" allows for one thing to represent another, and is most obviously necessary for the development of language. And finally, "deferred imitation" allows infants to display behaviors seen days earlier, a skill quite different from a younger infant's immediate mimicking of parental movement.

This development of symbolic or imaged representation formed the basis for not only language development, but also pretend play. For Piaget, pretend play was conceptually different from objective thought, in that it provided a "symbolic transposition which subjects things to the child's activity, without rules or limitations" (p. 87). He suggested that pretend play was nearly "pure assimilation," connecting one thing to another and, interestingly from a psychoanalytic perspective, "everything to the ego." So, the progression began earlier in year one: early, immediate perceptions and imitation provided the groundwork for internalization or "interiorization," which then supported and primed cognition for more sophisticated, symbolic, representational thought. This, in turn, supported a range of skills including deferred imitation, as well as reality-based and more "ludic" forms of pretend play. Importantly from Piaget's perspective, such were the seeds of intelligence and creative thinking:

> "This is why play is accompanied by a feeling of freedom and is the herald of art, which is the full flowering of this spontaneous creation." (p.152)

What can we say about Piaget's early description of what happens at the end of year one and into year two? How can we conceptualize what important and unique change has taken place? I will suggest that this shift from primary recognition and imitation of immediate experience to mental representation is analogous to being given a type of cognitive "workspace." In other words, it creates a secondary component of thinking where we can "set down" the objects we perceive or ideas we have and think *about* them, rather than only knowing of them in immediate experience. This is a central idea to understanding our hypothesis of autism, because as we consider mental representation in ever-expanding forms, from object to less tangible concepts, we are actually talking about "imagination" as we have defined it. Because you as the reader are an adult thinker who uses this secondary workspace continually and without effort, it may be somewhat difficult to conceive of life without it. But imagine (yes, you have to use the same ability I am suggesting emerges, to consider what it is like not to have it!) that objects did not continue to exist when you could not see them. Imagine not having a cognitive "space" to problem-solve, or maintain a word or phrase's meaning alternate to its literal one. Imagine your immediate experience engulfing the entirety of your cognitive functioning, with no optional "holding" area for reflection or cognitive manipulation. Imagine you could not employ the use of symbols or language. And imagine having no cognitive space to conceive of the mental states, emotions, or intentions of other people—that people would be a curious enigma that move in unpredictable ways and make sounds, only slightly different from everyday objects. These ideas may suggest in part, what the mental experience might be like for the person with autism, culminating in what we will see is a non-existent, distorted, or fractured sense or image of self.

Michael Tomasello

By employing concepts such as assimilation and accommodation, Piaget was able to hypothesize how an infant's developmental process proceeded as a result of his or her active, information-producing engagement with objects and people in the world. However, as noted previously, more recent research has shown that the infant comes into the world equipped with certain cognitive abilities that *precede* even the earliest manipulation of objects. Michael Tomasello has researched the manner in which these abilities emerge, and has shown how they correspond to early primate patterns (Tomasello, 1999). Further, he has proposed that there are a number of behaviors that emerge shortly after birth that demonstrate how human infants are distinctly different from their primate relatives. First, in the initial few months of life, infants engage in "protoconversations" with caregivers, which are shared visual, tactile, and vocal interchanges where emotional states appear to be communicated. Second, as was mentioned by Piaget, human infants as early as 3 months will immediately imitate head and mouth movements modeled for them, and by 6 months will even modify their behavior to match that of the model. Interestingly (and for later discussion), Tomasello suggests that these early forms of imitation indicate a "very deep identification process" (p.60).

While some might suggest that similar forms of these behaviors exist in the primate world, we turn to what Tomasello (and others) has dubbed the "9-month revolution." If there was any doubt that humans were cognitively different from primates at 6 months, this doubt is certainly erased by skills shown at 9 months. During the same period late in the first year when Piaget suggested "interiorization" or mental representation, Tomasello likewise notes that behaviors emerge that suggest a very different and uniquely human way of thinking. Specifically, in the months prior to the first birthday, human infants begin to engage in behaviors that include joint-attention, gaze following, and social referencing of the parent. These "referential" behaviors are soon followed by the related behaviors of pointing and showing, and as a group, come about in very close developmental synchrony. Tomasello suggests that these conceptually unique types of behaviors derive from a "dawning" understanding that others, like the self, are "intentional agents." That is, the infant begins to demonstrate via these behaviors, an understanding that other people have intentional "relations" to objects similar to the infant's own. As a result, the infant can, in many ways, now share with another in experiences. What were "dyadic" interactions with *either* objects *or* people now become "triadic" in that there emerges a "referential triangle of child, adult, and the object or event" (p.62).

But what is the underlying mechanism for these emerging,

distinctly human behaviors? Why is there a "dawning" and how does it take place? Clearly the absence of these important emerging behaviors is diagnostic for autism, and so it is essential to our goal of effective intervention to understand the precise trigger and process for the cognitive shift that occurs. Exactly how does this miraculous realization happen? Tomasello suggests that some sort of "simulation" operation takes place where the infant comes to appreciate that others are "like me," and un-like any relationship the infant has with inanimate objects. In other words, as the infant becomes increasingly aware of his own intentions toward objects, he assigns the same internal events to other people. As the infant becomes more aware of his or her internal states and emotions, he or she is interested in others because they "simulate" these internal workings. While there are similarities between these ideas and those suggested earlier by Piaget, Tomasello puts forth a much more specific mechanism or process—or does he?

Tomasello hypothesizes that 1) The infant becomes aware of his or her own intent toward objects in the world, and 2) Sees others performing (presumably) behaviors representative of the same intent, and 3) Infers that the internal, cognitive workings of other people are like the infant's own. But does this really explain the cognitive shift that has taken place? How does the infant come to be able to conceive of his or her own intent? Where does this ability to *think about* "intent" come from (since it is this imaginative ability that allows for the behaviors we see at 9 months)? It seems that "intent" is a concept that Tomasello is running on the same explanatory "tracks" that he may be attempting to create! By this I mean that one's own or someone else's "intent" is not something that can be seen or held; it must be imagined. Again, it is the emergence of this more abstract form of imagination itself that supports the distinctly human and "triadic" behaviors of joint-attention, gaze following, and social referencing.

The central cognitive leap that has occurred is that the infant has built upon or expanded his or her ability to imagine objects continuing to exist even though he or she can't see them, and now is able to imagine that others are "knowing," "thinking," or "intending."

We use this term "imagination" broadly as we first defined it, and I would suggest that object "imagination," for example, supports object permanence, and later intent "imagination" supports the behaviors representing the 9-month revolution. Tomasello all but makes this essential point:

> "…the child simply sees or imagines the goal-state the other person is intending to achieve in much the same way that she would imagine it for herself, and she then just sees the other person's behavior as directed toward that goal in much the same way that she sees her own." (p.76)

Our central question here becomes, what mechanism allows for the emergence of imagination capacities? This is a core question, but unfortunately as we have seen, Tomasello's "like me" simulation concept does little to provide us with answers. Perhaps, however, this was not his purpose—instead, perhaps the "like me" simulation was suggested to explain triadic *behaviors*, not the cognitive structures supporting them. However, Tomasello's writings in some ways do suggest a cognitive substrate. He discusses more complex imitative acts, the emergence of symbolic play, and perhaps one of the most complex representations of imagination, a concept of self later in his writings. In his own words:

> "…the human understanding of others as intentional beings makes its initial appearance around 9 months of age, but its real power becomes apparent only gradually as children

actively employ the cultural tools that this understanding *enables them to master…*" (italics added) (p.56)

Before we move on to other theorists who have attempted to tackle the cognitive shift of the 9-month old infant, we need to discuss two concepts related to our current discussion of Michael Tomasello's work. First, he uses a term that will certainly come up again in this book: "aboutness." Tomasello suggests that prior to 9 months of age, infants may perceive other people as animate objects that have the ability to "make things happen in some global way." But when an infant 9 to 12 months begins to understand and assign "intent," he or she is now demonstrating this "aboutness" in that, presumably, the infant is not only knowing, but now knowing "about." Similarly, we might say that we know a ball as an object if we see it, but it is something very different to say that we know "about" it. "Aboutness" suggests that we know perhaps physical properties of the ball, what it does or can do, that it exists even though we can't see it right now, and perhaps what it is not. When we switch from "knowing" to "aboutness," increasingly abstract imaginative capacities not only become helpful, they become essential.

The second concept has to do with the term "triadic." Tomasello and others use the term to explain the emergence of the referential "triangle" of child, other, and object—and it is contrasted with "dyadic." As we delve into this topic further, we will need a term to represent the imaginative capacities that come "online" at 9 months of age, and fortunately or unfortunately (depending on how you look at it), "triadic" fits the bill nicely. As we progress, the "triad" we discuss will not be child, other, and object, but rather child, other or object, and the thinking or imagination that holds the other or the object. For example, dyadic, "here and now" thinking of the 5-month old infant consists of child and other, or child and object. What exists is what is present at that moment in time. At 9 months of age however, imagination allows not only the child and the object or other to exist, but adds the third element of the triangle: existence of the absent object, or intent of the other person. You might be beginning to conceive now of this imaginative ability you have and how central it is to your functioning as a person. Can you imagine what would life be like without it? Or what would life and your existence be like if something went very wrong at this core step in the creation of your own human thinking?

Daniel Stern

The next theorist who has attempted to explain the shift in cognition that takes place is Daniel Stern, who is quite possibly one of the finest thinkers of our time. Stern (1985) takes a somewhat different view of the 9-month revolution than Tomasello, but you will notice a number of similarities, the most obvious being a "like me" concept. However, for Stern, the infant realizes the parent is *emotionally* similar, as opposed to being *cognitively* similar. In addition to the infant coming to understand that others have intent, Stern's theory accounts for an understanding of the caregiver's feelings.

Prior to the 9-month events previously mentioned, Stern suggests that the mother and infant are in a state of "core-relatedness." This term may sound like it is describing some type of close, relational bond between the two, but it is in fact, a basic, early, experiential sense that mother and child are physically *separate* beings. The infant is suggested to start at this point, which denotes separate affective states as well as histories. There is no understanding of the parent as having his or her own mind; rather, he or she is another thing or "agent" out in the world. The "quantum leap" that takes place toward the end of the first year of life is when the infant "gradually comes upon the momentous realization" (p.124) that thinking can be shared with someone else.

Stern acknowledges that these new abilities rest upon an entirely new set of capacities as compared to those needed for core-relatedness:

> "These include the capacities for sharing a focus of attention, for attributing intentions and motives to others and apprehending them correctly, and for attributing the existence of states of feeling in others and sensing whether or not they are congruent with one's own state of feeling." (p.27)

In a state of more sophisticated, shared, or *intersubjective* relatedness, communication is achieved through gestures, facial expressions, and related social referencing. The central event taking place that accounts for this leap is fueled by affective states that are confirmed by watching the parent's emotional response, or what Stern refers to as "inter-affectivity."

Stern proposes that this stage is critical to the creation of thinking and human development, and it is notable that he suggests what <u>may</u> occur in the event something goes awry. In Stern's words, "At one end is psychic human membership, (and) at the other (is) psychic isolation" (p.126). What else is autism if not psychic, and subsequent social isolation? At this point one may be wondering, what mechanism does Stern use to explain the emergence of the intersubjective perspective? He suggests the concept of "affect attunement," which has not been lost on autism researchers and theorists (e.g., Dawson, 1991; Rogers, Cook, & Meryl, 2005). In fact, Dawson (1991) has suggested that engagement in social interactions and the processing of novel and complex stimulus features necessary for affect attunement may be absent in persons with autism. Stern considers the emergence of affect attunement to be innate, and consists of a series of steps, beginning with the parent reading the child's feeling state accurately, and then performing an imitative behavior of that emotion. In return, the child realizes that there is affective correspondence or agreement, and finds the parent's imitative behavior enjoyable, so the reciprocal engagement continues. While this may appear to be similar to concepts such as "mirroring" or "affect matching" (and is to a degree), Stern focuses on the quality of *feeling* being shared, and less on the physical behavior itself. What is essential is a type of affective link that "can only be alluded to; it cannot be described (although poets can evoke it)" (p.27). Such words are reminiscent of Tomasello's reference to a deep, almost elusive, identification or joining with the parent.

For Stern, the shift to the intersubjective stage is crucial because it allows the infant entry into the psychological community. When the infant realizes that thinking can be shared with someone else, he or she has basically acquired "a 'theory' of separate minds" (p.124). In effect, Stern is saying that it occurs to the infant that what is going on internally matches what is going on for the other person, much like Tomasello's "like me" approach. However, the infant is not considered to be aware of any of these processes in any way that would suggest the ability to think about them in any "objectified" way. Rather this theory somehow opens the door to the psychological community by virtue of the subsequent emergence of skills: language, recall, symbolic play, and finally references to the self as an objectified entity. These skills typically emerge during the middle of the second year of life and later, and along with deferred imitation, are dependent on the need for a central skill: dual versions of reality, or the ability to imagine. The child develops the ability to represent objects not present, use words to represent objects, engage in true reality and the simulated reality of symbolic play, and both engage in behavior and represent cognitively their own execution of that same behavior. The typically developing child is able to move seamlessly between these various versions or layers of reality; he or she becomes able to think "about" objects (not just interact with them), events in time (not just the "now"), and not only who he or she and others are, but who or what they could be in an imaginary world. With time, the young child is able to conceive of the self as an object as evident through the use of pronouns, establishment of gender identity, and "acts of empathy" (p.165).

These emerging capacities are referred to as simply "imagination," but ultimately allow for what you and I enjoy cognitively on a continual, moment to moment basis. This process allows for complex, sophisticated, and mature perspective-taking, perception and prediction of intentions and expectations, and imagining alternatives both real and non-real. But have we really explained a mechanism by which all of these abilities come to be, or simply created names for the capabilities that are "realized," or "come about"? Does the parent performing matching imitative emotions really explain the emergence of the ability to "think about" any better than Tomasello's infant matching the intent of others to his or her own? Regardless of what you call it, thinking about, imagination, a second layer of processing abilities, intersubjectivity, or a term we will soon discuss, "meta-representation," none of the theorists so far explain *how* it happens; they give no actual process or mechanism, but do a beautiful job of telling us *what* is happening! Before we move on to the work of Peter Hobson, we need to mention Peter Fonagy, because his theory does tweak what Stern has offered just enough to give us some sense of what a true mechanism might look like.

Peter Fonagy

Much like Tomasello and Stern, Peter Fonagy and his colleagues (Fonagy, Gergely, Jurist, & Target, 2002) have suggested that similarities between the inner and outer world of the infant are at the core of the development of human cognition. Specifically, Fonagy argues that as the child expresses emotion, the parent reflects that same emotion in a "nearly, but clearly not, like me" manner. This theoretical orientation may look much like what Stern has put forth, but you will notice that it is not the "like me" concept that is central here; it is the "clearly not" portion to which we need to attend. When the parent imitates the infant's affect, Fonagy acknowledges that to the best of the parent's ability, the emotion of the infant will be "mirrored." But in reality, what the parent returns to the infant is clearly not a mirror image; it is slightly different in a number of ways. First, it is not the infant's image that the infant sees (of course), but rather someone else. In fact, it is likely to be a range of other people, because rarely does only one person interact with the child, and the instinct to mirror affect is a common one, even among the least parental of us! Second, the affect that is mirrored is likely to be an exaggerated version of the infant's and is delayed in time, so the infant expresses emotion and then slightly later sees a similar sounding and similar looking version of that emotion.

Interestingly, research tells us that infants prefer a bit of spice in their life, and will work for slightly novel stimuli to be presented. In fact, the form of mirroring or reflection described above is preferred over an exact reflection. Fonagy suggests that it is the *altered* parental presentation that has central value to the infant, but why? Imagine for a moment that someone has recorded your interactions at a meeting, because that person wants you to actually see how you behave. You think you are quite pleasant and cooperative at meetings, but after watching the recording, you see that in fact you are a bit pushy and need to have things go your way. Your first thought is likely to be something like, "Am I really like that?" When you ask that question, you are reflecting on yourself; you can see how the situation creates a sort of teaching environment that prompts a comparison of perceived self with real behavior. Now imagine what it must be like for an infant; these experiences are designed to prompt the very formation of the skill needed to figure them out. Fonagy calls this a "social biofeedback model" because the "nearly, but clearly not, like me" image provides a regulating or teaching environment by which the parent's affect can be internalized "through the establishment of secondary representations of the infant's primary emotion states" (p.190). In other words, having a similar but not matching model all but forces the infant to create, activate, or "bring online" a secondary processing system to accommodate the parent's affective information.

Unlike Piaget, Tomasello, and Stern, Peter Fonagy suggests an actual mechanism by which the infant develops this capacity to "think about." Fonagy adds to our growing store of "thinking about" terms by suggesting "secondary representations," which contain the *parent's* emotional information; thus the term "internalization." Similar to Tomasello's use of the term "identification," the infant is somehow "taking in" the parent because the parent offers similar, yet slightly different versions of the infant's own feelings. In essence, the parent's ability to imagine and then imitate the emotional expression of the child is guiding the emergence of the same abilities in the infant. As with Stern, the significance of this process is acknowledged by Fonagy:

> "These secondary representational structures will provide the cognitive means for assessing and attributing emotion states *to the self* that will form the basis for the infant's emerging ability to control as well as to reason *about* his dispositional emotion states." (italics added) (p. 202)

So it seems that we are a bit closer to our goal of understanding what happens early in life that forms the foundation for mature adult thinking.

To summarize, Piaget tells us that early imitation of another person leads to "interiorization" and lays the groundwork for "thinking about" or representative thinking in the forms of invention, symbolization, deferred imitation, and other more complex behaviors such as pretend play. Tomasello suggests that there is a dawning realization that others are "like me" and have the same intentions, that feeds the emergence of important triadic behaviors such as joint-attention, social-referencing, pointing, and showing. Stern and Fonagy agree that emotional reflection, imitation, matching, and engagement are essential components for typical cognitive development to occur. Both agree that these processes are foundational to the cognitive ability to form representations, think about, create non-realities, or any other term that relies on the general ability to imagine. We could conceive of the work of these monumental thinkers as a group: It would seem that we have consensus that just before the age that autism can be identified, some interpersonal event or set of events sparks a very different way of thinking. This more sophisticated thinking has been described as the emergence of mental representations, mental workspaces, the ability to *think about*, or duality of thinking, and allows for 1) early behaviors that the absence of is diagnostic for autism, and 2) later behaviors that the absence of are representative of autism symptoms later in life. I am suggesting that to varying degrees, the same cognitive substrate that supports joint-attention for the young child allows for the later creation of the highly complex concept of self. In other words, this leap in thinking early in life is the source of "I," or for the person with autism, *almost* "I."

Before moving on with this theory, we will turn to how these theories have impacted research on autism; not only from the perspective of typical 9-month abilities often being impaired or absent for the child with autism, but also in terms of one of the primary and most obvious set of behaviors supported by imagination: pretend play.

Chapter 4: The Real Victims in Autism: Imagination, Symbolism, and Pretend Play

Let's take a moment to summarize where we are in trying to better understand autism. We have discussed the standard diagnostic features of autism in the social domain such as early impairment in eye-gaze, joint attention, and shared enjoyment, which with time evolve into problems with social conventions, personal insight, and understanding the emotions of others. In the communication domain, impairments range from no speech to unusual speech to (later) poor conversational skills. In the repetitive or restricted interest domain, symptoms range from motor mannerisms ("hand-flapping") and a fascination with parts of objects, to an inflexible focus on (or discussion of, if there is speech) one topic. In addition to these more well-known symptoms, there are unusual symptoms that don't seem to fit anywhere in this triad of domains. They include things like impaired pretend play, impaired use of pronouns, unusual sensory responsiveness, and/or aggressive or self-injurious behaviors. For the diagnosis to be made, the triad group of symptoms need to be present before age 3, but of course there is a need for early identification of the disorder so that early intervention can take place. However, it is difficult to identify a child much younger than 1 or 2 years of age as having autistic symptoms, but some infants with autism do show extremes in temperament, no response to social smile, and a preference for non-social stimuli. As we look back on what we have covered so far, I want to point out the overall non-interest in social engagement that is rather obvious, and remind the reader about repeated, direct, and indirect references that show up with regard to "objects" or "things." There is an early, general disinterest in social engagement, accompanied by a preference for non-social stimuli, which is a fancy way to say inanimate objects. Related to this is also an often "mechanical" communication style, and a tendency to use others as "tools" in interactions. In the same vein, there is a fascination with "parts of objects."

Furthermore, we know that currently no known single gene or set of genes has been identified as the cause of autism. While there are some similar genetic patterns in a small sub-group of persons with autism and genetic indicators such as males developing the disorder more than females, environmental influences are also clearly evident and these must be active in the first year or two of life. Treatment that has shown some effectiveness involves active, intense, and high-frequency engagement with other people. This engagement focuses on increasing measured and targeted behaviors found to be lacking in the child with autism, such as eye contact, functional communication, and attention. In addition, we are interested in the behaviors that create the "9-month revolution" in thinking, not only because of the timing of this event, but also because the skills that mark this event are in many ways, the inverse of the symptoms of autism (joint attention, attending to facial expression, shared interest, showing, etc.). Taken as a group, one way to characterize these skills is that the infant has started to "imagine" in a very broad sense of the word, or that the infant has started to be able to think "about" things. Specifically, it seems that the infant comes to imagine concrete objects (as in object permanence), and then typically moves on to more abstract things, like object function or the emotions/thinking of others, laying the essential groundwork for progressively more complex and sophisticated skills and abilities. I want to be very clear here:

> *Considered in this way, imagination, defined as the*
> *generation of mental images, representative symbols, or*

61

thinking concepts, is the skill that supports a full continuum of abilities that may be absent to varying degrees in the child with autism across the lifespan. These skills are primitively demonstrated early in life through image-based object permanence, and extend to imagining such things as the concept of intent or emotion of another (corresponding to the 9-month revolution behaviors). Later in life, these skills may provide a means for symbol-based language and imagined alternative reality of pretend play, and open the door to more sophisticated dual-thinking abilities such as empathy, shame, and the concept of self. As the child ages, the area of impairment becomes more sophisticated (as you will see below), but the core source of the impairment remains constant: the ability to "think about" or imagine.

In other words, I am suggesting that virtually all of the symptoms that create the complex disorder of autism, both the standard and the not-so-standard symptoms, can all be conceived of as impairments in the ability to "think about" or imagine. One simply needs to try to conceive of them from this perspective. It may be helpful to summarize some of the imagination-based or meta-representative skills and behaviors that I am suggesting emerge early in development, and then continue to become evident in different ways as the child ages. However, note that not all symptoms are typically present in the child with autism, and there are many varied presentations and degrees of the disorder:

Skills Based on Early Meta-Representation or Imagination	"Thinking About" Skill Needed	Typically Impaired Absent in Autism
Object permanence	Imagination	Variable
Functional object use	Representation	Yes
Response to name	Symbolization	Yes
Social Referencing	Theory of Mind	Yes
Pointing/use of gesture	Theory of Mind	Yes
Joint attention	Theory of Mind	Yes
Social initiation	Awareness of other	Yes
Shared enjoyment	Theory of Mind	Yes

Later Associated Skills

Language	Symbolization	Variable
Recall	Representation	Yes
Deferred imitation	Representation/recall	Yes
Use of pronouns	Symbolization	Yes
Shyness	Awareness of other	Yes

Pretend/symbolic play	Imagination	Variable
Concept of past/future	Representation	Variable

Associated Skills of Childhood

Perspective-taking	Theory of Mind	Yes
Acting on the other's ideas	Awareness/Interest	Yes
Embarrassment	Self-representation	Yes
Humor	Symbolization	Yes
Coy behavior	Self-representation	Yes
Lying	Representation	Yes

Much Later Associated Skills

Self-reflection	Self-representation	Yes
Object of other's thought	Self-representation	Yes
Subtle social conventions	Symbolization	Yes
Concept of "self"	Representation	Yes
Problem-solving	Hypothesizing	Yes
Hypothesis creation	Representation	Yes

Finally, theories we have discussed to better understand the mechanism for the root development of the ability to "think about" include Piaget's "interiorization," Tomasello's "intentional agent like me" perspective, Stern's "affective attunement," and Fonagy's "like me but clearly not me" idea. While each of these theories has its merits, all rely to a great extent on the infant simply "realizing." The theories do not provide much in terms of explanation for *how* the actual supporting thinking structures may be built or created, which is what we need if we are to theorize what goes awry in autism and develop targeted intervention systems. Moreover, while each of the theorists in some manner suggests that autism is related to not successfully navigating the 9-month revolution, few have linked these formative ideas to autism as much as Peter Hobson.

Peter Hobson

In this next section we will discuss Hobson's contribution to this area, and then turn to a behavior that most everyone considers the "holy grail" in representing imagination: pretend play. While it may be difficult to conceive of object permanence or joint attention as forms of imagination, few behaviors so clearly exemplify the combined image-based and concept-based forms of imagining as pretending. Not surprisingly, this behavior is typically impaired in the child with autism, and for all of these reasons has received a great deal of attention, often controversial, from researchers. But first, let us discuss the work of Peter Hobson whose work I reviewed at length in previous published articles (Woodard & Van Reet, 2011). Hobson (2002) was interested in how infants shift from one way of thinking to another toward the end of their first year and into year two. He also discussed at length what could go wrong with a child's thinking, specifically and repeatedly citing autism. Early in this work, Hobson clearly states this idea:

"Centrally and critically, autism reveals what it means to have mutual engagement with someone else. It reveals this by presenting us with the tragic picture of human beings for whom such engagement is partial or missing. The autistic child's lack of emotional connectedness with others is devastating in its own right, but also has quite startling implications for the child's ability to think. These implications are what enable us to see how thinking itself is born out of interpersonal relations." (p.5)

In his descriptions of early behavior, Hobson notes that the very young infant is typically highly attuned to the social behavior of others, and as we have noted previously, is able to imitate others and is generally interested in the faces of others. The infant typically engages easily in the mutual, emotion-laden interchanges of mother and child, but interestingly, these social behaviors are accompanied by the non-functional use of objects (e.g., banging a toy phone rather than any approximation of its intended use) and interest only in objects that are present in the infant's environment. So, while there is a strong and basic emotional connection, thinking remains very dyadic, singular, and immediate.

As year two begins and then progresses, the infant starts to show the types of behavior that are indicative of what we have been calling the 9-month revolution: the infant gestures to communicate to the parent, shows items to the parent, points, and becomes more interested in (and typically consistent with) the parent's affective response to events. Hobson suggests (as have our other theorists) that a clear step in thinking sophistication is now evident, but at this early stage of the cognitive progression, the infant does not yet realize that others have minds of their own. In other words, although these behaviors as a group do not signal an infant's understanding that the other person has a mind of her own per se, there is a foundational, new form of triadic "about-ness" in thinking:

> "Objects and events can be communicated about. Or, to put this another way, the infant's interactions with another person begin to have reference to the things that surround them...These events reveal that infant is no longer restricted to a focus either on an object or a person, but instead may be sensitive to a person's relation to an object." (p.62)

In a sense, the infant is becoming more and more aware of the uniquely separate behaviors and thinking of other people as time goes on. A basic awareness of others and objects as having the potential for a relationship with each other has begun to emerge; the infant is no longer as limited to "here and now" thinking, and we see again the now familiar cognitive leap to thinking "about." But how does Hobson explain what is happening and what does he think is taking place? Hobson suggests that certain supporting behaviors such as imitation of others and assumption of their attitudes take place "automatically"—and these behaviors create the foundation for the later emergence of abilities such as consciously chosen perspective taking. But for now, the infant is only aware that there are others in the world with information, and the infant watches them, imitates them, and assumes their emotional reactions, because the infant is "innately equipped" to do so.

For Hobson, the next steps in how thinking develops are marked by a growing sense of self and others, language, and symbolic or pretend play. Reviewing all of these areas is beyond the scope of this book, and as noted earlier, we will focus on pretend play. It is not that language (as a form of representative symbols) or a conceptualization of self are not good examples of the ability to think about or imagine—it is simply that pretend play provides one of the best and clearest examples. Pretend play embodies some interesting terminology that is related to concepts we have proposed, and has received research attention that may be of help in better understanding autism. Hobson discusses "object substitution" as one form of pretend play, when a child allows one thing to "stand for" another. For example, a banana "becomes" a telephone, or a rock "becomes" a car. This type of behavior suggests that the child is now able to conceive of objects in a very different way. The child can not only understand what the object is, but also what the object *could be* (but is clearly not). As pretend play progresses, the child may choose to draw in an adult to share in the pretend event. This act demonstrates a real deepening of simple awareness of the psychological stance of another, in that now there is the beginning of an acknowledgment that this other person has an active mind of their own with a variety of functions and facets. The other person is now perceived as having volitional ideas, desires, and wishes of their own, and these can be real or imagined; the child can use these, reconstruct them, and integrate them into interactive, reality- or fantasy-based, spontaneous play.

Think of it! In just one year, dyadic, here-and-now thinking and interactions with objects and people have developed into the ability to think *about* them in a non-real way. The resulting information and understandings can be, and typically are, then shared with others. As year one progresses, the infant builds upon these base abilities and becomes able to depart momentarily from reality into a generated, imagined world. They can then effortlessly rejoin reality. The child can simultaneously maintain a concept of reality and one of non-reality, and can move seamlessly between the two. Others can become part of this world, and soon evolve into active players with imagined ideas and roles of their own. Note that for Hobson, the early base abilities are linked to and support other subsequent events as we have noted above, such as thinking about the self as a self, shyness, and embarrassment. These demonstrate the child's further cognitive extension into the ability to conceive of the self as the object of another's critical evaluation. But as far as pretend play is concerned, what is proposed by Hobson (and other theorists) about this gold-standard behavioral marker of the emergence of "about-ness" thinking needs to be compared to what research tell us. While it might seem like we are veering off-track slightly, this is an important set of ideas that we need to consider for just a moment. We will then come back to Hobson's mechanism for how all this thinking evolution takes place.

What We Know About Imagination and Pretend Play

Few behaviors are as representative of imagination or symbolic thinking as pretend play, and the "how and why" of early pretend play has been a central focus since the time of Piaget. What is the purpose of pretend play? How does it happen? Why does something so apparently confusing and non-adaptive as creating a non-reality serve a child in a positive way along a developmental trajectory? As we have noted earlier, impairments in pretend play are diagnostic for autism, and even its presence in these diagnostic features is riddled with confusion. Under which domain should pretend play be considered? Is it a social behavior? Is it a communication behavior? What does impairment in this area mean for a child with autism? What does it tell us about what is happening internally or psychologically for this child? As early as the 1970s and continuing into the 1980s, researchers were already asking these questions. Wing, Gould, Yates, and Brierley (1977), for example, were some of the early researchers who defined *functional* play as the use of objects (including miniature versions of objects) as they are typically intended—for example, a little teacup is used as one uses a teacup, or a play phone for a phone. By contrast, *symbolic* or *pretend* play (these terms are used

69

interchangeably) was defined as object substitution, that is, imagining objects not present ("drinking" from a cup when no cup is actually present), or imagining specific properties of an absent object. The early research generated by Wing et al. (1977) and later researchers (e.g., Mundy et al. 1986) suggested that children with autism were able to engage in some degree of pretend play, but the play was less spontaneous and complex compared to typically developing children. In addition, the play was much *more repetitive* (or less varied) in children with autism compared to typically developing children.

At the time, the concepts used to explain pretend play (and then by association and extension, the concepts proposed to be impaired in autism) were "primary representations" and "meta-representations." In Leslie's (1987) theory, a primary representation was defined as a depiction of the world in an "accurate, faithful, and literal way" (p. 414). However, exactly what a primary representation was and how it differed from a perception, image, or memory is not clear. There were many other authors who also used this term—including Perner (1991)—but they provided equally unsatisfying definitions: "A representation is something that stands in a representing relation to something else" (Perner p.18). It may be that Leslie simply had created another word to lay the groundwork for the dual-thinking model we have been discussing. Sure enough, Leslie subsequently suggested that during the second year of life, a "meta-representational" mechanism developed in addition to "primary representations." For Leslie, meta-representations were defined as "not representations of the world but representations of representation" (p. 417), and these versions could be altered or reconstructed. In fact, meta-representations allowed for the capacity to actively imagine, and generate a range of indefinitely reconstructable mental images or concepts. Obviously, the meta-representations could deviate in fundamental ways from primary representations of the real world, at the whim of the person doing the imagining. Leslie's specific mechanism for this was that the infant developed the ability to "decouple" (or separate) the primary representation from reality by creating the "meta" copy of it. The infant thus developed the ability to suspend reality and engage in pretend play by creating and manipulating the meta-, decoupled representation while at the same time leaving the primary representation of reality intact.

Leslie theorized that autistic children are not able to form meta-representations (although he did not suggest a reason for this impairment), thus causing their documented pretend-play deficit. However, during the 1980s and into the 1990s, more and more research began to challenge the meta-representational model as an explanation of autism. For example, Lewis and Boucher (1988) found that *high-functioning* children with autism (mental ages averaging around 5 years) were able to engage in pretend or symbolic play equal to that of typically developing children. This finding threw the whole concept of meta-representation into question, and the same authors even replicated this research in 1995 (Lewis and Boucher, 1995). What was interesting about this controversial research was that the children with autism did not engage in pretend play *spontaneously or with novelty*; they needed to be cued and pressured to engage in pretend play. More research that followed (e.g., Charman et al. 1997) found similar results, suggesting that something other than a deficit in meta-representational thinking was perhaps at the core of autism. Unfortunately, most of these studies used "high-functioning" participants as noted above, which further complicated what the findings meant, and what could possibly be going on to cause the emergence of autism.

Theory of Mind as an Expansion of Meta-Representation

The concept of meta-representations was initially exciting because it provided researchers a way to explain autism that most people could understand. It was relatively simple and intrinsically appealing to a variety of researchers (e.g., Happe 1994; Frith 1989), and it explained a great deal of behavior related to autism. When research emerged that contradicted these ideas, the challenges were reluctantly acknowledged because some had expanded upon the ideas dramatically. One of these researchers was Baron-Cohen (1996) who had proposed that meta-representation allowed people to imagine and understand the minds of others. He called this process the development of a "theory of mind"(ToM). In his book on what came to be known as "mindblindness," Baron-Cohen suggested that typically developing persons develop the ability to imagine or cognitively represent the states of mind of others. This can then be extended to imagining states of mind of the self during insight or self-reflection. Simply put, ToM allowed someone to "think about" the human states of mind. The model for ToM that Baron-Cohen developed became a complex and comprehensive four-component system. It began with an "*intent* detector" and an "*eye* detector" that combined to create "triadic representations," which culminated in mature ToM. To explain the source of these skills, Baron-Cohen posited they were the outcome of a long, evolutionary process, and then the subsystems leading to ToM simply came "on-board." For persons with autism, something went awry in this progression though it is not clear what. To demonstrate an impaired ToM in persons with autism, Baron-Cohen used the "Sally Anne" task. This research technique involved moving items without certain characters knowing they had been moved. Baron-Cohen et al. (1985) found that most, but not all, children with autism were unable to correctly assume the mental perspective of the various characters in a story. Similar to the research in pretend play, certain children with autism were able to perform as a typically developing child would although the majority of the children with autism tended to respond incorrectly, in a "non-thinking-about" manner rather than a meta-representational manner.

Given the variability for persons with autism on the Sally Anne task and variability in pretend play, where does this leave the meta-representational model? If one conceives of meta-representation (or for that matter, imagination as we have defined it) as an "all or none" ability and hence the mechanisms that allow for the creation of imagination need to be either on or off, then we can dismiss the whole idea of meta-representation as being the core of autism because clearly, some children with autism can demonstrate some form of these behaviors some of the time. But what if it was not an "all or none" ability? What if one could develop these abilities to a degree? Is it possible to develop a little imagination? And if so, how would it happen and what would it look like?

Back to Peter Hobson

The work done by Peter Hobson provides an excellent example of the emergence of more and more sophisticated levels of mature thinking, and what this might mean for the child with autism. For Hobson, the very young, typically developing infant is naturally highly attuned to the social behavior of others, and he or she is continually watching, gazing, and imitating the immediate behaviors of those around them. Then there is a dramatic shift in thinking at the end of the first year of development and into year two, signifying a real change: the infant is now able to think about objects with the parent in a referential way, gesturing, showing, pointing, while both referencing and taking on the emotional attitude and responses of the parent. Awareness of the other person's intentional and emotional relation to an object comes "online"—or, in other words, the infant can now begin the process of developing the capacity to imagine the thinking and emotions of other people, laying groundwork for a host of other skills that rely on this ability, including pretend play, empathy, language,

73

embarrassment, and a concept of self ("I"). Not coincidentally, all of these skills, including those seen early in life as well as those that develop later in the typically developing child, are impaired in the child with autism to various degrees. Hobson suggests that the typical infant is "innately equipped" to perform certain early behaviors and maintain emotional connectedness with the parent—and he provides us with a mechanism or process by which this entire evolution in thinking takes place: identification.

In the next chapter, we will discuss what the concept of identification is, how it is related to the psychoanalytic (Freudian) school of object relations, and why identification has been generally disregarded in the field of autism. It turns out that researchers in the field of autism have a pretty good reason for avoiding identification, but we'll discuss more about that later. Hobson (2002), on the other hand, had no problem presenting this concept as central to the development of thinking, and therefore central to autism. Consider this quote:

> "More than this: thinking arises out of repeated experiences of moving from one psychological stance to another...The mechanism by which all this occurs is the process of identification...To identify with someone is to assume the other person's stance or characteristics...The critical element in this kind of identifying I am describing is that it involves feelings and attitudes. This kind of identifying does more than change a person's actions – it changes the person's subjective experience of the world." (p.105)

Hobson (2005) further suggests that identification creates the mental space for more complex levels of thinking, and that it is precisely this process that causes the problems seen in persons with autism:

"By means of this process of identification in the context of triadic person-person-world relations, they are lifted out of their one-track, inflexible perspective to apprehend things and events 'according to the other.' This process is not only critically disrupted in children with autism, but also critically important for the development of context-sensitive symbolic thinking." (p. 417)

As a cautionary note, we need to be careful about how we are conceiving of this deceptively simple process called "identification." Even in the above passages, it is not entirely clear what is happening. Is the child actively and naturally assuming or taking on the "stance" of another, or is the child being "lifted" out of one-track thinking by some external force? What actually happens in the process of identification? Understanding this concept is important because it is suggested that due to this process of identification, the infant comes to see that the parent perceives the infant; the infant then realizes that he or she can be the object of another person's perception. What this creates is a self-awareness-based form of thinking, and the ability to perceive the self as an object of evaluation, which leads to things such as embarrassment, shyness, or coy behaviors demonstrated later in development. Simply put, it is the (usually) "automatic" process of identification that allows for the creation of the mental space to think about, which underlies so many other skills yet to be developed in the child. As Hobson (2002) states:

"It is because what is internal becomes external, and what is external may be internalized, that relationships can promote the development of a capacity to think, even in adulthood." (p.175)

Chapter 5: One Way to Explain It: Identification

It seems like a simple enough word, identification, yet it is really quite a complex concept when one examines its history in psychology, and more specifically within psychoanalysis and the related schools of thought that have emerged from Freud over the years. We will discuss this in more detail later, but for the moment, think about what identification might mean to the layperson. As we mentioned above, the term was used by Hobson to mean the assumption of the "stance" or "characteristics" of another person. But when used in everyday conversation, it often has a wider meaning. For example, you might say to someone, "I can identify with what you are saying," meaning that you can easily imagine or understand the other person's perspective or line of thinking. Or you might say, "Our group is identified as conservative," meaning that your membership is unified in an idea or ideal. Identification has many related terms such as "identity" or "identical," which in its own right implies a unified sameness or oneness. As a group these terms suggest that identification can mean more than a similarity between two things—it can infer an actual unification, where two entities are actually considered one and the same thing. Or consider this somewhat different definition that is more in line with the form of identification we are interested in:

> "A largely unconscious process whereby an individual models thoughts, feelings, and actions after those attributed to an object that has been incorporated as a mental image." (Merriam-Webster's Medical Dictionary, 2007)

Interestingly, this definition is from a medical dictionary where identification is subsumed under the psychoanalytic perspective, the traditional orientation of psychiatrists. Notice the part about the incorporation of a "mental image" which truly resonates with our discussion so far and some of the ideas and concepts that we have covered. A psychoanalytic orientation is synonymous with Freudian ideas, but this is actually an area that has evolved over time and taken many twists and turns since the early part of the 20th century—so many in fact, that we need to limit our discussion to one of the most recent and significant incarnations of Freudian ideas, the school of "object relations." For readers whose practice orientation is the more common behavioral approach, I understand that what I am discussing here is about as far from how you have been trained as we can get. But autism is a complex disorder that requires all of our collective fields and expertise if we are going to fully comprehend what is happening. To this end, I find it necessary to make full use of ideas from varied schools of thought.

Before we move on to this area, the definition above shows another problem with terminology in discussing identification within object relations. In this instance, the problem comes with the word "object," which most people understand to be something inanimate, like a brick or a spoon. In psychoanalytic circles, the term "object" is used more broadly to mean the aim of a psychological drive, usually the person to or with whom another person is relating. In other words, an object is usually a person, and what is of interest here is how that person-as-object is identified with and incorporated into another person's psyche. Incorporation can and does create the "mental image" of the person noted above, or more importantly, the internal representation of the relationship with that person-object. As defined by Michael St. Clair (1996), an object is "the 'other' involved in a relationship or, from an instinctual point of view, that from which the instinct gets gratification" (p.219). Nevertheless, the object being a person is not an absolute, and there is actually no clear requirement in psychoanalytic theory that an object must be a person. This truth is plainly stated in one of the most widely cited texts on the various schools of psychoanalytic thinking, Greenberg and Mitchell (1983). This means that from a psychoanalytic standpoint, an object could, in fact, be many things including an inanimate object, or in the more traditionally Freudian use of the term, it could be a person. In fact, in discussing the complex process of identification in detail, Schafer (1968) notes:

> "The subject may, of course, identify with representations of nonhuman creatures and things as well as with those of other persons. Identifications with pets, wild animals, and machines, to give a few examples, are not rare." (p.142)

This is an important point because as we have seen, the process of identification has been suggested to play a central role in how we develop the ability to think. Thus, knowing *how* we are identifying may be as important as knowing with *what* we are identifying. If how we think is derived from what we identify with, how would thinking change if the identification "object" was just that; an inanimate object and not a person?

How "object relations" fits into therapy

What is the role of an "object" within the context of Freudian ideas called "object relations"? Note that theorists have made many changes to Freud's original ideas over the years, and the school of object relations is just one such interpretation. While people commonly think that psychoanalysts are mired in Freud's original focus on sexuality and the id, Freudian thinking has actually quietly moved on and continues to be the core training mode for psychiatrists and many psychologists. In the school of object relations, early experiences with parents create an important template or lens through which we all understand or see our own world. For better or for worse, the idea is that how we related to our parents and how they responded to us as children lays the foundation for how we function later with other "objects" or people. Simply put, as we grow older, those very early relationships are acted out in our adult relations. For example, let's say that as a young child, you secretly resented your father's over-bearing and authoritarian "pushing around" of your mother and other people in your life. As you grow older, when you encounter persons in authority (like a teacher or a boss), your tendency is to re-enact this early "object-relation" with your father, and you might inappropriately challenge or obstruct this person for reasons you don't understand. Anger would quickly and easily rise to the top in these types of situations, and you would not be able to enjoy a neutral and balanced emotional response. This type of problem would be a common one that someone brings to therapy, asking, "Why do I do this? It is causing so many problems in my life…" Because the answer is hiding in the way that person was trained early on to see the world, the obvious answer remains a mystery to that person without assistance from the therapist. That patient's own psychological "tracks" are part and parcel of who they are—so much so that they can't see what is happening. One of the goals of therapy based on object relations ideas is to illuminate these patterns, so the patient can become aware of what he or she is thinking and doing—and why. Once the patient is aware of where the emotion comes from, he or she can more easily work through the associated emotions and decide whether or not to change the pattern.

While most people think that an analyst is going to ask a lot of questions about your past and/or early childhood (which he or she may do), it is actually the novel and new encounter with the therapist that is of central interest. Just like our relationships with others, the patient begins quite naturally to weave the same types of relations with the neutral therapist, re-creating bits and pieces of earlier "relations" with past "objects." Presented with this very unusual relationship, the patient acts in the manner known best to him or her, creating "transference" that the therapist notes and considers. By this term, we are describing the process by which the early emotions of the patient are transferred to the therapist and become fodder for the therapeutic process. In essence, the therapist "becomes" that mother or father in that the patient's early feelings, thoughts and behaviors felt or acted out in the therapist's direction. As the patient continues to "transfer" his perspective onto the therapist, the patterns brought forth illuminate the patient's general take on the world, other people, and even his relationship with himself. The very manner in which the patient functions psychologically is exposed through this process, and the skilled psychoanalyst acknowledges it, understands it, and in time, gives it back to the patient in a way that (hopefully) leads to insight, understanding, and subsequent improved functioning for the patient. This is not a simple process, and the therapist must be careful to avoid opening a wound that cannot be closed. In addition, the therapist has to manage the patient's thinking and behavior, as well as his or her response to the patient. This "counter-transference" can provide important information about the patterns that are becoming evident, but the core idea is that what is enacted with the therapist represents what the patient felt and experienced as a young child. Being able to put these emotions and thoughts on the table in a safe environment will lead to growth. So, the idea that how one experiences the world early on in life influences how one thinks and feels today bears some vague resemblance to what we have been discussing up to this point— that early relations with others might create the very manner in which we think. Have psychoanalysts considered this idea? It turns out they have.

The Ugly Psychoanalytic Past of Autism

One of the reasons that psychoanalytic theory has been largely neglected in research on autism and its treatment has to do with an early psychiatrist, Bruno Bettleheim, who, in the 1960s and 1970s unfairly and incorrectly blamed the emergence of autism on the mother. If you know about or have seen the movie on Temple Grandin, you know of tremendous damage that can be done by assuming such a stance. But in the latter part of the last century, we knew very little about autism, and it was rarely diagnosed compared to today. Bettleheim proposed that autism was the result of the mother withholding sufficient affection from her children, resulting in a poor emotional connection. The father was also blamed but to a lesser degree, mainly due to his weak or ineffectual presence in the child's early life. None-the-less, the blame fell squarely on the shoulders of the parents, resulting in the popular term "refrigerator mother." The theory basically suggested that the emotional "coldness" of the mother was at the core of autism—and these unfounded ideas remained a central explanation for autism for many years. Despite the fact that there were typically developing children present in the families of a child with autism and that there were mothers with warm, compassionate, and caring personalities, this theory became popular and the damage done remains a hot-button topic in autism research and treatment. In fact, while the essence of the observation-based, behavioral model is antithetical to abstract, internal, psychoanalytic approach, this does not capture the intense resistance to and common derogation of psychoanalytic thinking in many autism circles. In my experience, any reference to these ideas is at best met with skepticism and suspicion, but more often with outright rejection. But when one considers the damage done by putting forth such ideas, this type of response is understandable.

While I am certainly not a proponent of Bettleheim's archaic ideas, I am also not ready to throw out the proverbial baby

82

with the bathwater. Instead, let's begin at the beginning and re-focus on the psychoanalytic concept that may help us better understand autism—identification. Freud introduced the idea of identification in the early 1900s (Freud, 1917), and then expanded the idea in later revisions of his theory. One of the best explanations he gave of identification was in his famous introductory lectures (Freud, 1932), where he described it as a type of assimilation in that one person becomes so like the other person that it was as if one was taking the other "up into itself" (p.63). This characterization would again suggest more of a type of unification or merger, where one person was not only "like" the other person, but temporarily actually *is* the other person in a way. This notion extends beyond Hobson's conceptualization of identification as the assumption of "characteristics," to include the very *being* of the other person. Such an idea is hardly news to the psychoanalytic community, as psychoanalysts such as W.R.D. Fairbairn (1941) suggested a nearly complete merger with the parent at a very early age, or in psychoanalytic-object terms, a "state of identification with the object." Interestingly, not only have psychoanalysts in the recent past focused on identification, but they have also delved into the 9-month revolution in thinking ideas that we have been discussing, albeit in a characteristically abstract manner. For example, a renowned psychoanalyst, Edith Jacobson (1964), talked about the role of objects in the development of infantile thinking at exactly the point in development with which we are concerned:

"As the child enters his second year of life, changes in the nature of his relations to the object world set in…they mark the introduction into the psychic organization of a new time category, the concept of future. Moreover, they presuppose

83

the ability to distinguish…differences between objects—
animate and inanimate—as well as between objects and the
self." (p.49)

Jacobson's position was that the process of identification—and the
object with which the individual identified—typically replaced the
state of most primitive self and other fusion, and that the resultant
self-image was a function of the internalized traits and parts of the
other person or object (Fonagy & Target, 2003). She continues
later in the 1964 volume, to discuss how the process of
identification also leads to ever-expanding sectors of the
developing mind:

> "Object and self-awareness grows, perception and
> organization of memory traces expand. The object imagery
> gradually extends to the animate and inanimate world.
> Language symbols, functional motor activity, and reality
> testing develop." (p.53)

In addition, consider the following discussion of how symbolic
thinking derives from early emotional experiences from Otto
Kernberg, one of the best-known object relations theorists living
today (quoting Otto Kernberg in Sandler, 1987):

> "Shifting from consideration of the minimal requirements for
> the assumption of symbolic thinking to that of the
> development of a subjective sense of self, I have proposed
> that this development may be conceived as taking place in at
> least three stages: (a) an early state of primary consciousness
> or subjectivity, first activated during peak affect states and
> characterized solely by affective experiences without any
> sense of self; (b) a later stage of self-awareness, that is, a
> reflective awareness of a subjective state that differs from

other subjective states, and (c) an integrated sense of self as the basis for a self-reflective awareness of any particular subjective state—the 'categorical self' of the philosophers. Self-awareness is now not only that of temporally changing subjective experiences while a 'self looks on' but a clear awareness of a continuous entity of subjective self as something stable against which each subjective state is evaluated." (p.97)

For Kernberg, identification results ultimately in the formation of self or the "I," modeling itself on the selected object, which is typically the parent (Fonagy & Target, 2003). We know that psychoanalysts have been thinking about thinking for some time, and creating theories for many years that touch upon how early experiences create the psychological world of the infant.

Because one of the main goals of psychoanalysis was to provide an effective form of therapy, the role of ideas such as those noted above was often of secondary importance. Usually they were of interest only to the extent that they supported or informed what was happening in the adult mind. If psychoanalysts were interested in what happened in early childhood, it was often only because it helped them understand the roots of adult borderline personality disorders, depressions, or psychotic conditions. In fact, direct links between early development and disorders that emerge later in life are common in psychoanalytic literature (e.g., Horner, 1984). Even our central concept of identification was considered commonly (although certainly not exclusively) serving child development a bit later than the 1- to 2-year-old age range we have been discussing. For example, identification with the mother or father formed basic sexual dispositions as an outcome of the Oedipal process that was considered active during year three to year five. This is not to say that identification was not active during earlier formative years, only that it was a different kind of identification, sometimes called "primary identification" or what Kernberg called "introjection." Remember that in discussing autism, we see problems in developing imaginative functions or "thinking about" that emerge late in the first year of life and then become more apparent into the second year when a clearer diagnosis can be established. Because of this, any discussion of identification needs to be quite early, primary and basic, based on what is evident or hypothesized during year one.

Part-object, whole-object identification and where autism comes in

So, what is this thing we are calling primary identification? Primary identification is a particularly chaotic and affect-laden state, where the self and object (usually the mother) are considered "non-differentiated." Simply put, this means that during this stage of identification, the child does not merely assume the "characteristics" or "stance" of the object, but is in fact, one with the object temporarily. This is considered an early state of unification or "merger" with (usually) the mother, where she or another significant caretaker functions as the organizing or holding psychological vessel for the infant. (It is actually the process of secondary identification where the infant takes into the self-representation the more commonly considered characteristics or attributes of the object (Sandler 1987).) It is this primary identification that results in the creation of the infant's framework for the genesis of his or her subjective world; the infant's formation of their own self-representation via the "taking in" of the maternal "object." The famous psychoanalyst Margaret Mahler (Mahler et al., 1975) suggested a similar form of identification when she proposed that the very young infant became "symbiotic" with the mother, or quite naturally enters into an undifferentiated

86

physical and psychological state with the mother. The symbiotic "dual unity" of mother and child laid the very foundations of healthy thinking and personality functions:

> "Within the symbiotic common orbit, the two partners or poles of the dyad may be regarded as polarizing the organizational and structuring processes. The structures that derive from this double frame of reference represent a framework to which all experiences have to be related before there are clear and whole representations in the ego of the self and the object world (Jacobson, 1964). Spitz (1965) calls the mother the auxiliary ego of the infant. Similarly, we believe the mothering partner's "holding behavior"… is the symbiotic organizer—the midwife of individuation, of psychological birth." (p.47)

Successful unification and attachment with the mother preceded later "hatching" or psychological separation in the second year of development, from what Mahler called the "symbiotic orbit" of mother and child. Healthy and successful navigation of this process resulted in strong psychic structures that came to represent what was "self" and what was not self. In other words, identification is much more than one entity deciding to being similar to, take on characteristics of, or be "like" another entity. From a psychoanalytic standpoint, primary identification means, at least during very early development, that child and parent are psychologically one dual unit—and while they are one, parts of the basic roadmap of how to think, feel and manage the world are transferred from the parent as object, to the child. This is an important idea because it means that the type of identification we are interested in involves the child more or less *becoming* the "object" with whom (or with which) the child identifies. In other words, the child becomes able to think as a result of the early, successful identification process, and so the process of identification becomes as important as the actual object selected.

Before we move on, it is important to touch on one other aspect of primary identification with the "object." In psychoanalysis, the taking in of an object is often thought of as progressive—sometimes from a "part-object" state to a "whole-object" state. This is easily understood when applied to later development, when only certain aspects of objects are perceived. For example, a young person or adult may be able to see only positive or only negative aspects of that other person. Not surprisingly, this creates problems because they are not conceiving the "whole" person or object as it really is, just the parts they can tolerate or comprehend. Sometimes this is referred to as only being able to see the world and the people in it in "black and white," rather than being able to accept that people are mostly "shades of gray." People are almost always combinations and degrees of opposing traits—they are good and bad, cooperative and obstructive, loving and unkind. In psychoanalysis, a mark of successful and well-functioning development is being able to see people in the world as "grays," whereas seeing only certain aspects of people is a defensive function designed to keep out ambivalence that might overwhelm a fragile psychological system. This defensive function is sometimes referred to as "splitting," although this term has other meanings and applications as well.

What we are interested in is a much earlier and much more primitive application of this concept. This line of psychodynamic theory suggests that even very early development typically proceeds from part- to whole-object understanding. In the stage of development that we are concerned with, namely primary identification where the infant temporarily is the parent psychologically, the part-object for the developing infant might be a bottle or human body part, such as a breast or hand. (This concept always reminds me of one of the diagnostic behaviors of the child with autism; using the hand of another person as a singular tool or thing, rather than a part of another person.) This understanding moves on to a "whole object" orientation, where, for example, there is a more complete or more inclusive and whole father, mother or other object. This perceived whole-object would have a range of human properties as noted by Fairbairn (1954). Another psychoanalyst, Schafer (1968), talked about this part to whole process further when he wrote:

> "Psychological development includes increasing ascendency of the secondary process: object representations…tend toward complex differentiations…they tend toward objective wholeness in the sense of encompassing and organizing enough significant physical and psychological attributes of an object to constitute a substantial, specific, and enduring human figure…" (p.144)

So, what happens if you consider the idea of part- to whole-object understanding during the very early stage of primary identification? We already know that the very young infant "is" what they identify with, which may or may not be a whole human object. In the chapters that follow, I will suggest an alternative theoretical explanation derived from these ideas that better integrates what we have learned about the symptoms of autism, how thinking develops, and more discrete behaviors and skills such as pretend play and symbolic thinking.

As we discussed previously, research has not fully supported the representational/meta-representational model of autism. The present psychoanalytic approach might better explain what we know about autism by expanding upon Hobson's concept of identification, specifically, as I have stated previously (Woodard & Van Reet, 2011):

"Primary identification is a process by which the very mind of the infant is constructed by the object, nonliving or living, with which he or she identifies. The 'stuff' of identifications is derived from the perceived world of the infant, or the objects that are in fact nonliving things and people. Note, however, that even people are, from an analytic orientation, perceived first in part-object form; it is only with transitional time and integration of the person as a whole-object that understanding evolves from a collection of things or parts to a living being that has the capacity to imagine. We propose that the distinction between an inanimate object and a whole human object is central to how the typically developing mind is structured and created, given these voluntary imaginative functions or abilities of the whole human object." (p.220)

In other words, identification involves the developing infant psychologically becoming that person or thing with which he or she identifies. Further, if the developing infant does not navigate completely from a part-object to a whole-object orientation, as most infants quite naturally and easily do, he or she will hence perceive the world and the self in the manner reflective of the degree of this progression: ultimately the creation of "I" or in the situation of autism, almost "I." That is, if the child chooses, for whatever reason, to identify with an inanimate object instead of a person, and/or only identifies to a limited degree with a person on a part to whole progression, *so will his or her thinking be*. And as you know, inanimate objects can't imagine or "think about" like people can; only people are able to do that.

Chapter 6: Identification with Inanimate Objects: The Absence of "I"

We have now discussed many of the essential ideas necessary for proposing a new theory of autism based on the concept of identification. We have discussed the main and associated symptoms, as well as enough about genetics and treatment to leave us a bit perplexed as to what autism is, where it comes from, and how it evolves. We know that there is simply no single gene that leads to the expression of autism, yet there are certainly genetic forces at play. We know that behavioral treatments have only moderate effects—mainly because the etiology is so poorly understood. However, the timing and nature of the disorder have led us to focus on the 9-month revolution in thinking, the period in development a number of researchers in the area of autism suspect to be of central importance. But how is this early process related to autism? What actually happens to cause this disorder? Is there some semblance of ideas or concepts that we can use to at least get a basic understanding of what is happening? The theories that seek to explain the 9-month revolution in thinking are complicated not only by their abstract form (thinking about thinking is not easy), but also by the challenges of infant development research and the fact that so many different things are taking place at the same time as a child grows. But as a group, they suggest that what we consider normal human thinking is derived from a certain type of pervasive, early relationship with the world—specifically, early relationships with people in the world. Because these types of concepts are far beyond the reaches of the predominant behavioral perspective, we need to venture into areas traditionally "off-limits" to researchers in autism. While undoubtedly unpopular, we need to draw upon a perspective based not on what is seen and measured, but rather on what is abstract, non-observable, and purely psychological conceptualization, supported only by what we think the infant is thinking.

Why we need to meld behavioral, developmental, and psychoanalytic theory

Because the area of autism research is dominated by a behavioral orientation, this approach might be a hard pill to swallow. However, if we are to move forward, even if some might feel this is a step backward, we need to expand our exploration into areas that may very well have something to offer alongside a solid functional behavior analysis. The area of purely psychological conceptualization that deals in the period of development we are interested in is the psychoanalytic concept of identification. We have discussed how we are less interested in the more common secondary type of identification, and more focused on earlier, primary identification. It is during primary identification that the parent and child psychologically and emotionally unify, and create the bond or relationship that some developmental theorists believe is so unnamable that only a poet or painter could actually capture what is happening. It is this period of primary identification that I am suggesting is central to the emergence of autism—not only due to the closeness in timing to when we see autism first emerge, but also because it is during primary identification that certain aspects of the early templates of thinking are hypothesized to be forged and provided to the infant via symbiotic joining with the parent. That is to say that the choice of the object identified with and the extent to which whole objects are integrated into thinking over part-objects, makes an important and unique contribution to the overall process of core, "thinking-about" cognitive development. This is first evident in the infant, and then can continue to affect thinking and behavior as the person continues to mature across the lifespan.

To be as clear as possible: to make further progress in understanding autism and related treatment, or at least to create a theory that can suggest testable hypotheses, we must meld behavioral, developmental, *and* psychoanalytic thinking. This takes current thinking, that effective autism treatment must draw on behavioral concepts and techniques, developmental theory, and the natural social context, and adds a much more abstract set of ideas. We can draw upon the major contribution of the psychoanalytic school to the extent to which psychoanalysts have conceived of, as Margaret Mahler puts it, the psychological birth of the human infant. More specifically, I am suggesting that:

For a variety of reasons, the infant on the trajectory for autism comes into the world with a propensity or preference for inanimate objects and part-object identification as compared to human object and whole-object identification. These are not mutually exclusive states, but better conceived as a continuum of identification options. Primary identification contributes to the emerging cognitive structure by influencing interactive components: 1) how we understand, conceive of, and perceive of the world around us, and 2) the level of complexity or sophistication in how we think "about," which is derived from the extent to which a whole human object is chosen. These factors affect not only thinking and associated behaviors in infancy and across the lifespan, but also how we conceive of abstract concepts such as the self. Thus, the spectrum of autism disorders is, for all intents and purposes, an outcome of variations in the process of identification and subsequent impairments to the early thinking "about"/imaginative capacity. The infant's propensity for the inanimate and part-object end of the continuum may be sufficient for autism to emerge, or may be further propelled by environmental factors. This means that

94

1) influencing elements would be any genetic or environmental factor that influences or contributes to placement or movement on the hypothesized continuum, and 2) treatment would be effective mainly to the extent that placement or movement towards the human/whole object end of the continuum is achieved.

That being said, we can proceed by first delineating what this supposed continuum might look like as a stand-alone concept, and then as it relates to autism. Next, we will look at extensive supporting evidence as to why this continuum might be a reasonable way to conceive of autism. And finally, we will discuss one element that is hypothesized as contributing to the increased prevalence of autism: our continually increasing cultural obsession with objects.

Identifying objects vs. people

In my 2011 article (Woodard & Van Reet, 2011), we discussed the continuum that I will here again propose. However, here we can expand on it more fully. We suggested in 2011 that the inanimate to human object concept needed to be considered in concert with the idea of part-to-whole psychological development. These awkward terms are, at present, the best we have to convey the main thrust of this area, and are complicated by the fact that even people are, at first perceived in part-object form. It is only with time that a person potentially comes to be understood by the infant as a whole person or unit. But what do we mean by a "whole" person? How can we better understand what leads up to this typical and normal state of identification? I have suggested that it might make more sense to begin in this uncharted theoretical territory with four main demarcations of identification as follows (with acronyms slightly altered from the original):

1) Part-object/Inanimate object (PI) Identification (least sophisticated)
2) Part-object/Emerging Human (EH) Identification
3) Incomplete Human (IH) Identification
4) Whole Human (WH) Identification (most sophisticated)

We will discuss each of these possible forms of identification on the continuum in turn, first from a general theoretical standpoint, and then in terms of how each might further explain what is seen in autism. This discussion builds upon what was only outlined in the 2011 article.

The first form of identification (PI) suggests that the infant, for any number of possible reasons, has oriented toward part-objects and inanimate objects, and away from human objects, for identification. Interestingly, a similar observation was made by Margaret Mahler more than 30 years ago, but never fully developed. Mahler (1979a) notes that, in what she calls autistic infantile psychosis, the mother "remains a part object, seemingly devoid of specific cathexis and *not distinguished from inanimate objects*" (italics added) (p.135). She continues, "This autistic psychotic child was characterized (as were all those whom I observed) by a peculiar inability to discriminate between living and inanimate objects, even in a perceptual sense" (p.138). Mahler (1979b) even provides an example of non-human identification during the symbiotic phase in her case presentation of Harriet, and the mechanical outcomes:

"As early as at 8 months, she consoled herself and enjoyed nothing more than rocking back and forth before a large mirror in an autoerotic fashion, watching herself and thus reinforcing the kinesthetic sensations… Her preference for inanimate objects over people was striking. Her

96

identifications were with dolls, or at best, with the family dog... The not-yet 14-month-old little girl seemed to oblige mechanically." (p.115)

Given what we know about identification, what else could we hypothesize identification with an object looking like? Most obviously, there would be a general interest in things as compared to people, although if an aversion to the sound or presence of people was present, inanimate objects would likely be far preferred over people. To the observer though, even an equal level of interest in things and people would likely appear to be, as compared to typical development, an unusual disinterest in people. Further, it would be sensible to assume that certain things could be attached to and appear nearly obsessional in their importance—like how a typically developing infant clings to the mother, an infant with this hypothesized PI level of identification would cling to things. With respect to the idea of the identification object creating the manner in which we see the world, every object in the world (including people) would necessarily only have inanimate object status. In other words, things would be things and people would be things, because the uniquely human thinking properties had not developed in the early identification process. The infant who remains at the PI level of identification could and would perceive the world (both objects and people) in the most basic inanimate object form, and the capacity for understanding the unique qualities of living things, such as volitional thought and emotion, would not emerge. Thus, both things and people would be *treated* as if they were things— and both the child's relationships with things and with people would be emotion-less and mechanical.

It does not take much imagining to think of what this might look like for the infant progressing through the end of the first year of life and into year two: 1) equal interest in or a preference for inanimate objects over people, 2) the treatment of people as if they were objects, 3) the treatment of other living objects as things (i.e., the family dog), and 4) an absence of interest in the indicators of thinking and emotion in others, namely behaviors such as joint attention and social referencing. As a side note, I am unclear on how this course of events would affect object permanence. At first, I suggested that because it is an imagination-based skill, meaning it is dependent on human identification, a PI level of identification would bar its emergence. However, it is also a skill that uniquely emerges prior to the 9-month revolution in thinking, suggesting that it may be a skill somehow unique in psychological, thinking development. Perhaps research in this area would clarify the role of object permanence: exploring if there is a difference between object permanence skills in the most severely autistic children (those with no spoken language, absent reciprocal socialization, and repetitive behavior) as compared to those less severely affected. I suspect the answer would be "yes", which would suggest that the identification process is having the expected effect on this skill area. However, a "no" answer would support its unique properties, perhaps related to the pure object qualities and developmental timing of this particular skill area.

Returning to the idea of everything in the environment as having only "thing" status—to imagine this, we would have to conceive of all living things with only mechanistic or robotic qualities. Note that we need to use the real kind of robots in this exercise, not the emotion-laden, humanoid ones often represented in movies. All the living things in our world would move and do this or that, but without any emotion or voluntary original thought. If you or I came in contact with one of these "machines," we would likely treat it as such; we might touch it or turn it, or use it as it is designed to meet our immediate needs, but that is all we would do because we understand it to be a thing. Or, we might ignore it if it bears no particular use for us at this time. We understand that you can't insult a machine, so we would simply go on our way. This thing might only be of interest because it does move or it can do something it is designed to do, but beyond that, it is simply an object in our environment with certain features of interest that many of the other objects do not possess. Now let's imagine adding to this exercise that we know these "robots" are not machines, but rather living beings with original thinking and emotion. Because of this, the person at the PI level of identification would perceive these particular "robots" as inconsistent and at times, unpredictable machines. They would, by their very nature, violate many of the rules of "things" by behaving differently for any number of reasons (e.g., a new thought on how to do something, an attempt to substitute one thing for another, the result of a change in emotional state, etc.). It is understandable that this shift might make people a bit aversive to the child with autism who perceives people in the world in this manner—how long would you want to stay around your unpredictable robot?

When I say "the rules of things," I am referring to the physical rules that one would expect the child at the PI level of identification to use to conceive of the world. Things typically do not move on their own, change form or shape, come or go on their own, or use original thought or emotion to guide their behavior— that's what makes them *things*. Once typically developing infants recognize behavior that indicates this particular type of thinking and emotion—the kind that humanized, emotional robots have, they would become fascinated with the prospect of a thing crossing over to having uniquely human thinking. This may be what makes for a good sci-fi story, but at the PI level, we would conceive of an expectation of constancy, for everything from my lamp today being a lamp tomorrow to having things in a certain formation. But we need to be careful not to move into the next level of identification which allows the person with autism to base rules of constancy on how things "should" be; this denotes a primitive ability to think "about," which is not present in this most basic PI level. Constancy for this level of identification would need to be limited to how one knows the world to be, based on memory and experience, rather than a more categorized, comparative, or conceptual knowledge of how it "should" be. After all, memory is not necessarily affected by the identification process, but rather limited by the level of thinking sophistication that results from the identification process. In other words, much like associative learning remaining basically intact but limited, memory would continue to function within the confines of an absence of the ability to think "about." It would be more of what we think of a "recognition" memory, and less of what would be "recall" memory—the person would know something when they saw it, but pulling the idea up in one's mind and reconstructing it or altering it from the original would not be possible. This idea may become clearer as we continue our discussion on what a PI level of identification means to the process of thinking and the emerging concept of self.

For the person at the PI level of identification, one would expect that changes from or alterations to the original of any number of things might be alarming, but we can also conceive of how they might be fascinating. For you and I to conceive of some version of this, imagine both our amusement and our dismay when we watch a magician do things that we know to be physically impossible. The more rule-violating the trick is, the better the act. But now remove from the equation your knowledge that it is only a trick performed by someone whose job is to create illusion. Suddenly the experience becomes both amazing and a bit unsettling, if not downright terrifying. Much like the robot that has become unpredictable, violation of the rules of the physical environment has the potential to confuse, worry, and alarm us. At the PI level of identification, this response is not because we are afraid of what "could" happen as a result (that would again require thinking "about"), but because what we know to be one way is suddenly different—it is "incorrect." It does not take much to imagine the continual state of stress that might quickly ensue with a PI level of identification. I would suggest that this concept is one source of the high stress we see in persons with autism as they develop.

In addition to these factors: 1) things and people being of equal importance, 2) people being conceived of as things and treated as such, and 3) a severe and essential preference for constancy, I would expect that the PI level of identification would be marked by a fascination with *parts of things* rather than the whole. Our theory suggests that an object orientation is associated with "part" versus "whole" conceptualization, which would lead one to expect that individual parts of things (which include people at this level) might bear special interest. Objects as things in what you and I consider to be whole form would not be perceived by the person at a PI level of identification. Rather, they would have an interest in sections, portions, or parts of things, and we would expect them to seek these parts out: a hand would not be part of a whole person, a button would not be part of a larger toy, and a doorknob would not be part of a door. These would all be individual parts, each bearing their own level of importance or significance—and they would be treated as such. How would this look behaviorally? There would be an interest in what you or I consider to be unusual details of a thing or a part that typically one would ignore or perceive only as serving a subordinate function to the entirety of the object like a doorknob, button, or hand. Interestingly, if we begin to combine aspects of what we would expect a person with a PI level of identification to be, we can start to picture how this person might behave. Pairing constancy with a focus on the parts of things, for example, would suggest this person might tend to engage with parts of toys that do the same thing over and over. For example, this person might spin a tire on a toy car continually, rather than use the car as an integrated whole,

101

and use another person's hand as an unconnected "tool" in the environment. These are exactly, by the way, what clinicians look for in early tests for autism.

Primary identification and the concept of self, or "I"

Beyond these four likely and more obvious outcomes of primary identification with an object instead of a person, we need to consider how such identification might affect two additional, inseparable concepts: 1) the level of sophistication of thinking and 2) the concept of self. I have suggested that the type and nature of the object chosen for early identification affects not only how we perceive the world as noted above, but also the level of complexity or sophistication of thinking. This is a broad statement given the many functions and skills that we consider to be "thinking," but our theory is made a bit simpler by being able to delineate what makes people so different than most other (dare I say all?) inanimate objects in the world: people think "about" or "imagine" and they have emotions linked to this ability, as we have previously discussed. As evidenced by behavior, many aspects of thinking are well underway even at birth and shortly thereafter (e.g., recognition memory, the capacity for associative learning, habituation, and even a basic understanding of the physical rules of the environment), and would not be inhibited necessarily by inanimate object identification. However, the unique contribution that can be made by *person*-as-object (the ability to think "about" and the experience and understanding of associated emotions [associated because they too must be imagined]), would not be available to the person at the PI level of identification. Such a situation could have devastating central effects on the person experiencing this trajectory, and a multitude of secondary effects. Keeping this fairly abstract idea in mind, we can hypothesize how a PI level of identification would affect certain aspects of the person's cognition.

Beginning with early development, the ability to think without the commonly associated ability to think "about" would further propel the infant's disinterest in joint attention and social referencing because the capacity for conceiving of another person's thinking, purpose, or intent would be virtually absent. Similarly, there would be no purpose in following the eye-gaze of another person or pointing out something of interest because other people are not perceived with the capacity to think "about." There would be no social smile or shared enjoyment with another, because the infant at the PI level does not have the capacity to imagine the enjoyment or emotion that the other person is experiencing. Facial expression of others would be inconsequential, because the emotions of others can't be imagined. More specifically, for the infant at the PI level, emotions generally considered related to or derived from relationships with other people would be absent. This is not to say that the person at this level would not have emotions any more than they would not have the ability to think; they would simply be emoted in response to events related to things rather than people, or purely organic experiences such as internally derived mood. As the infant began to develop further, the absence of the ability to think "about" would necessarily bar the emergence of functional play following stereotypical use of objects, and pretend play would be absent because this behavior is acutely dependent on the ability to imagine. Furthermore, any cognitive function based on symbolization would be out of reach, as these types of abilities require the ability to have one thing "stand for" or represent another. Without this ability, the infant at the PI level would not respond to their name, and spoken language altogether would be tremendously challenging if not altogether impossible. However, because associative learning remains intact, a person at the PI level may appear to understand some language to the extent that certain verbal expressions of others have led to positive reinforcement or punishment consequences that could be drawn from available memory. The more sophisticated emotions of the young child that are dependent on thinking "about" relationships with other people would not emerge and feelings of empathy, shyness, guilt, coyness, or embarrassment should be completely absent.

Beyond these early manifestations of the absence of the ability to think "about," later emerging, dependent, and related cognitive capacities would be affected. For example, the concept of time would remain a complete mystery to the person at the PI level, because the past and the future do not actually exist and must be imagined. Interestingly, this does not mean that there would be no recognition of things and people from the past—just that the experience of existence for the person at the PI level would be, by necessity, an ever-present "now." For this reason, concepts such as waiting or linking current behavior with much delayed, future consequences would be difficult. What "could" happen, which is dependent on both the concept of future and the ability to imagine a variety of outcomes, could not be comprehended. The ability to hypothesize, problem-solve, or "look forward to" would be absent. Also absent would be worry about future events and fear of what "could" happen, which might initially sound comforting, but one can also imagine the stress of not being able to hypothesize what is likely to happen "next." Further, because it cannot be imagined or integrated as a whole concept, the idea of a physical or psychological "self" would not be possible. The bodily self would simply be a curious set of physical things that are continually nearby, completely disconnected from the absent whole concept of there being a "me." Imagine what a sensory experience would be under these circumstances—experiencing a surprising sensation, but it coming from nowhere and being a part of nothing. My leg would not be "my" leg, because there is no me. As a result, what happens to it is likely to be of little consequence, perhaps only until pain or other physical sensation is registered, if it is registered in this situation.

Likewise, the concept of the psychological self as you and I experience it—the concept of "I" or "me"—would be absent for the person at the PI level for a number of reasons. First, the concept of "self" is an imagined concept that we build by integrating parts, two functions that we already know are incapacitated at the PI level. Second, the early creation of a concept of self is thought to be the result of a culmination of the early thinking "about" skills: the infant not only imagines another person thinking "about" and feeling "about" other things, but the other person is also thinking about and feeling about *me*. Therefore, there must be a "me." The ability to conceive of a psychological "self" or concept of "me" is clearly acutely dependent on and derived from the early ability to imagine the thinking and feeling of others, and so it is not something that the person at the PI level would be able to create. Much like the curious notion of recognition memory existing but absent a concept of past, or having emotions but not those derived from relationships with others, the concept of self would be consciousness without the "thinking about"-dependent elements that you and I are so accustomed to having alongside consciousness: self-awareness, self-concept, and the ability to self-reflect. In other words, the person at the PI level would "be," but would not perceive the self as an existing entity that can be thought "about." But how would we know that a person was functioning in this manner? In addition to the markers discussed so far, I would suggest that, for example, the person at the PI level of identification would have virtually no ability to comprehend death—there would need to be a "me" for there to be the possibility of no "me." However, they may notice that someone is

105

no longer present. It would also be extremely challenging if not impossible for this person to describe himself or herself as a self, or communicate in a way that indicates what he or she is "like," or how he or she tends to "feel" from day to day or moment to moment.

We have discussed a series of indications or expectations based on a PI level of identification: people are perceived as things, on equal par as things, and treated as things without thought or emotion; there is likely a preference for constancy; parts are more interesting than wholes; and cognitive development is impaired wherever thinking "about" is needed. There is little doubt that this set of expectations is beginning to sound a bit familiar to the reader who has any experience with autism. Still, there are three additional levels of identification postulated: Part-object/Emerging Human (EH) Identification, Incomplete Human (IH) Identification, and Whole Human (WH) Identification. What happens when there is some movement along the hypothesized continuum?

Chapter 7: The Identification Continuum and Emergence of "I"

The PI level of identification is hypothesized to be the most extreme end of the continuum, noted for a nearly complete absence of identification with a human object, an absence of the perception of the whole human object, and an absence of the initial emergence of the ability to think "about," which is suggested to be derived from the human object's unique, same ability. This ability to think "about," or intersubjectivity—a second layer of thinking, dual-processing capabilities, or meta-representation—is barred at the PI level as a result of early inanimate object unification and identification, rather than identification with a human. Without psychological unification with a whole human object that has thinking "about" capabilities, we would not see the linked behaviors that typically emerge during what is known as the 9-month revolution. As noted previously though beyond this most absolute level, we would hypothesize three more main demarcations: Part-object/Emerging Human (EH) Identification, Incomplete Whole Human (IH) Identification, and Whole Human (WH) Identification. What might these look like? The next level of identification, the EH level, suggests that inanimate object identification was not absolute, and that some early placement on or movement on the hypothesized continuum took place. At this level, the infant or child would have a less absolute part-object orientation, and due to partial identification with a human object, he or she would be able to think "about" to a corresponding degree. The many areas touched by the ability to think "about" would be less severely affected, and a wide variation of abilities could emerge as a result. This would therefore result in a somewhat less severe presentation of autism, and perhaps also open the door to a more optimistic response to treatment. However, this is unknown at present, and the only way to determine the validity of such a statement would be to conduct future research.

Part-object/Emerging Human (EH) Identification

To better understand what this might look like, we can follow the same descriptive path created in the previous chapter. Note that with a more complete discussion of the PI level, my discussion of the EH level has evolved somewhat from the original journal article. Theoretically as a result of partial human identification, there would be a somewhat increased interest in other people, perhaps as a special type of thing or a thing with special qualities of movement, a giver of reinforcement, or a most basic understanding of intent. But interactions would retain, to a great degree, the mechanical quality of the PI level. Primitive thinking "about" abilities might allow for basic emotional bonds to certain, select others that would be most apparent when this person was in their presence, but not as apparent when not in their presence. Difficulty with early separation from a caregiver would likely only be apparent for a very short period, if at all. There would likely remain a preference for constancy and repetition, but we may begin to see early evidence of the ability to adjust to alterations with lessened distress. There would be a reduced focus on parts, or perhaps a beginning integration of wholes, meaning the presence of select understanding of how things go together or work together. The EH level would suggest that the developing infant would show minimal joint attention and social referencing, but continue to rely mainly on recognition memory skills. Emotionally there might be emerging or select instances of shared enjoyment, and sporadic interest in the facial expressions of others. Note that in all these hypothesized areas on the continuum that are here being discussed, there would be the possibility of significant variation, but this theory would suggest that such skills and behaviors would emerge in concert with each other.

The ability to think "about," even to a basic degree, would have significant effects on the developing young child in that very primitive and impaired dual-processing becomes possible. While again, there would be significant room for variation, the young child at the EH level should begin to evidence primitive or sporadic functional play as compared to solely stereotypical play. There may be some ability to engage in basic or rehearsed pretend play, but the quality would be poor and engagement would likely remain limited, non-spontaneous, and stilted. Most significant at the EH level of identification would be the potential for basic language, but this also would vary greatly in terms of quantity and quality. As with pretend play, language might be awkward, rehearsed-sounding, or otherwise unusual. Because there is only the basic ability to think "about" at the EH level, language related to physical qualities of the environment should be more easily grasped than the abstract, other-person-based qualities, such as emotion or "my" (speaking as the other person) likes or dislikes. Because there would remain an unrealized concept of self-as-object derived from more advanced comprehension of the thinking of others, language would likely be marked by an absence of, or confusion regarding, pronoun usage. "I" or "me" or "you" would continue to have virtually no meaning in the world of the person at the EH level of identification. Similarly, emotions would likely remain a general mystery due not only to the need for intact thinking "about" capacities, but also the other-based nature of emotions. Those emotions generated by or derived from relationships with others—shyness, empathy, guilt, or embarrassment, for example, would remain out of reach for the person at the EH level. Only the most primitive or basic comprehension of emotions (happy, mad, sad, etc.) may be possible.

As the child became a bit older, the availability of partial thinking "about" capacities would allow for minimal comprehension of concepts such as **time**. For example, the person at this level of identification may be more able to understand "waiting," but more complex versions of time such as, "We will be doing that in three days," or, "You need to wait until 4:00," would remain a frustrating and complex conundrum. At the EH level, we might see problem-solving abilities in the most basic form, and select instances of fear stemming from recognition memory of feared stimuli. There would be a primitive comprehension of the body as a more unified thing or object, and disconnectedness of body parts as unrelated units would diminish. However, the more advanced, other-derived concepts of self-awareness or self-reflection would remain absent. The body may be a somewhat more unified, physical object, but it could not as yet be thought of in an objectified manner, or the object of another person's thinking. Therefore, the full concept of "self" would remain elusive for the person at the EH level. One other interesting and generally uniquely human quality that might relate to the level of identification would be the presence of **humor**. Considering the PI level of identification in comparison to the EH level, we would imagine that the person at the PI level might laugh mainly in response to sensory stimulation or internal states. Any humor related to dual meanings ("I was wondering why the baseball got bigger and bigger, and then it hit me") or even when things are different from how they should be (such as wearing a funny hat), would of course be lost on the person at the PI level. Whereas with a person at the EH level, we would expect much the same although there would be the possibility that a rudimentary understanding of physical object or "slapstick" humor may emerge.

Incomplete Whole Human (IH) Identification

At the third hypothesized level of identification, the Incomplete Whole Human (IH) Identification level, expanded human and whole understanding is accomplished. This level of identification would allow the developing infant an improved yet incomplete capacity to think "about" or imagine—and better integration and understanding of wholes versus parts. So, how might this level of identification manifest itself? With these improved abilities and capacities, other people could now be perceived as having some concrete thinking capacities, although the more abstract and complex human emotional functions would be more challenging to comprehend and work with. There might be a better understanding of the more basic emotional states in others and the self, but subtle or complex emotions would still be difficult. There would be a clear and preferred understanding of inanimate objects, and while there might be a remaining preference for constancy and repetition, there would also be an improved capacity for flexibility and accommodation to alterations or changes. The person at the IH level would likely want to indulge their thinking and preference for objects, and focus on inanimate object interactions despite an improved awareness and understanding of people as able to think and feel. Related to this idea, some researchers have suggested that high-functioning persons with autism have been able to use parts of the brain typically devoted to object processing for face recognition, instead of using the facial cortex (Scherf et al., 2010). The infant at the IH level would have joint attention with others, but still prefer to focus on objects versus people. Some notable social referencing and eye-gaze following should be present, however. There should be improved shared enjoyment, although it might also derive from objects. Some emerging coyness and shyness, as well as stranger anxiety could be present at this level of identification.

A young child at the IH level would have the capacity to

engage in functional play, and would understand how parts come together to form a whole to a great degree. This would likely be apparent for object wholeness as compared to people, meaning a complete and deepened understanding of people would remain elusive. Pretend play should be present but not fully consistent with typical play behavior; inanimate objects and ritualized or repetitive play might be preferred over representations of people and play that considers or elaborates on social relations or emotion. Solitary pretend play may be preferred, and others would not likely be drawn into this play activity. Verbal capacities and language would be largely intact, although again, given the preference for objects and constancy, language might be marked by an object or topic focus and rigidity or repetition. Memory functions would have the capacity to develop some abilities to recall in addition to recognition memory, and problem-solving and hypothesizing would become a possibility. These functions might happen with inanimate objects as the main topic however, in comparison to people-based challenges. With thinking "about" in place to a greater degree, past and present would become available yet likely still be impaired concepts, and the person at the IH level would begin to be able to fear what "might" happen, especially as it relates to their physical existence. Similarly, the self could be partially conceptualized, but would remain mainly relative to physical object form or facts about the self, with the more abstract emotional qualities being curious, confusing, or simply a mystery. There would likely be limited and primitive self-awareness, and perhaps the ability for limited self-reflection if pressured with special challenges when it comes to one's own emotions. Embarrassment or the constant monitoring of other people's evaluation of one's own behavior, a common aspect of the typically developing child, would likely remain absent. We can quickly imagine the particularly frustrating, confusing, and even painful social existence of the person at the IH level of identification, although with intensive support, approximations of improved social behavior would become possible and have been shown to emerge (Lopata et al., 2010).

Whole Human (WH) Identification

Whole human (WH) identification would be associated with the typically developing person, and represented in what is known to be normal (meaning most common) progression in the areas discussed above. The infant would display the full thinking "about," imaginative capacities, and would understand objects and people in whole form. This means that people would become understood both as things existing in space and time in the physical world, as well as distinctly different from objects because they can think and feel. There would be an interest in objects, but a preference for people-oriented interactions and all the emotional indicators that this involves. Interactions with others would be marked by fascination and joy, and joint attention, social referencing, following eye-gaze, and shared enjoyment would emerge virtually effortlessly. There would be openness to spontaneity and change, the emergence of functional play and pretend play that integrates things and people, facts and feelings. Others would be drawn into this active play, and preferred over solitary play. There would be the capacity for fully symbolic thinking, normal language development, and the typical emergence of shyness, empathy, stranger anxiety, and embarrassment. The self would be, with time, understood as a whole being, as both a physical object and a thinking and feeling object, and there would be a natural sharing of these unique attributes with the people in their world. The capacity for understanding complex emotions in the self and others would emerge with time, as would the capacity to self-reflect and self-examine. And the continual monitoring of another person's cognitive and emotional response to one's

114

behavior would be present as it is in typically developing persons.

In effect, the WH level of identification would allow to emerge what we understand to be typical thinking "about" capacities, and all of the cascading abilities it affords. By using the ideas of co-occurring inanimate object to human primary identification alongside a part- to whole-object progression, and placing these concepts together on a continuum, one can hypothesize the early effects on infant development. As we move along the continuum, the shifting interest in (or focus on) objects and then people, the decreasing insistence on and then preference for physical object constancy, and the evolving part- to whole-object (meaning both inanimate and human objects here) understanding are all fairly easily conceived. A bit more challenging is imagining how these shifts or changes in the developmental trajectory would interact with the associated degrees of emergence of the ability to think "about," and how these combinations of events might affect cognition and be demonstrated from a behavioral standpoint. By having worked in the field of developmental disability and autism for nearly three decades, I understand that in describing this continuum and progression I may be influenced by knowing the "end of the story;" but I don't think that this minimizes the tremendous similarities between what may happen at the proposed levels of identification and what we know as the spectrum of autism disorders. In fact, it is the degree of progression on such a continuum that, for the first time, allows us to advance a theory that can accommodate the wide variation (and yet often common clusters) of clinical presentations seen in people with autism.

Note also the opportunities that this theory could create for autism research. Before using research findings to conclude what is or is not representative of autism, this theory would require identification of the severity of the participant group's disorder— has the researcher used a group that is best identified by a PI, EH, or IH level of identification and functioning? Vastly different findings would be expected based on this information and proposed system of categorization of severity. Confusion would certainly result from a "mixed" grouping that would likely lead to an uneven or non-uniform group response to interventions, a finding that is not lost on autism researchers, as we will see in the next chapter. While identification of cognitive functioning is somewhat helpful, the closest researchers typically come to addressing this issue is the occasional reference to the group being "low" or "high" functioning. The lack of a theoretical framework that is linked to and suggests a logical degree of impairment of the disorder of autism itself creates a significant blind-spot at one of the earliest steps in the research process.

The identification continuum and a newly conceptualized theory of autism

The effect that an infant's placement on the proposed continuum has on the behaviors that are representative of the 9-month revolution in thinking, and therefore the emergence of autism, should now be rather apparent from our discussion. How other-human-based behaviors such as following eye-gaze, eliciting attention from others or joint attention, shared enjoyment, pointing, and showing behavior would be absent or diminished, as well as a preoccupation with parts rather than wholes, and a desire for constancy, repetition, and ritual are all easily derived from this theory. Even empathy being absent, pronoun reversals, the non-existent or incomplete concept of self, impaired pretend play, and absent, unusual, or otherwise impaired language development begin to have a logical source. But what about the other, associated behaviors we mentioned in earlier chapters? Given our newly conceptualized theory, are these behaviors easily understood and explained, or would doing so be more of a "stretch"? Take for example, the tendency for children with autism to use others in a mechanical fashion, as tools in play, and using parts of other people's bodies in unusual ways. This tendency is commonly evidenced by the young child with autism when he or she places another person's hand on an object in a manner that does not indicate that the child is touching another human being. Instead of taking the other person's hand, looking in their eyes, and indicating some type of need, the child with autism picks up another's hand as they would a pencil, book, or other small, inanimate object. The behavior resembles someone using a set of automated tongs in an effort to get the object to grasp or move another object. Since our theory suggests that people are, to a great extent, conceived of as inanimate objects, this type of behavior is actually quite sensible from such a perspective. Recall our robot example. If your robot was having trouble grasping something, what would you do? You would take its "graspers" (whatever that might be) and help the robot along.

Similarly, we commonly see impairment in gestures for the child with autism. Gestures such as clapping, shaking a finger, or shrugging, are symbolic forms of communication learned only by attending to another person; infants are unlikely to come into the world equipped to shrug. Lacking an interest in the behavior of other people and an inability to think "about" (by letting a body movement represent a communicative meaning), gestures would likely not develop. On the other hand, with time, an older child at the PI or EH level may come to understand via associative learning that shaking a finger results in a punishment consequence and therefore with training, may inhibit this behavior in the presence of this discriminative stimulus. However, the use of this gesture and then understanding altered yet similar meaning gestures without training (raising a finger to gesture "wait" for example) would not occur.

In another example, a common diagnostic sign for autism is the child not responding to his or her name, or doing so inconsistently. I would suggest that, like the child showing minimal referential eye-gaze or minimal enjoyment in social interaction, there may be a significant differentiation between not responding to name and some responding to name: the latter would indicate progression away from the PI level and would be a positive indicator. But the reason for not responding to name is the same: First, the child needs to be interested in what other people are saying and, at the object end of the continuum, they simply are not; second, they need to know that one's name is a symbol for or representation of that self. At the object end of the continuum, neither of these concepts, symbolism or self, are present. Without these conceptual structures in place, why would a child at the object end of the continuum respond to a name? As with our previous example however, with time and training and consistent reinforcement, such a behavioral or rote response may become possible; but an understanding of a name as actually representing this imagined thing called "me"—a self with likes, dislikes, emotions, and relationships in the world—would likely remain out of reach. Similarly, the lack of using pronouns follows the same logic: if there were no imagination-based concept of "me" and secondary thinking "tracks" for symbolization, how would one be able to understand or use "I"?

Understanding other symptoms of autism

Another common symptom of autism is echolalia, meaning repetition of the last statements made by others. Similar to this, autism is sometimes associated with "scripting," which is seemingly meaningless or nonsense repetition of books, commercials, or other statements that the child with autism has heard. Sometimes these are repeated over and over, usually in a manner unrelated to anything going on around them. Can we use our theory to explain this phenomenon? This is an interesting example because we can use the theoretical demarcations to note that if this behavior is present, we are likely dealing with a child who is at the EH or IH level of identification. This is because the symbol-based skill of language must be present, so we would expect this particular symptom to be associated with the corresponding, improved levels of functioning in other areas (some functional play, some increased awareness of and an interest in other people beyond the object level, and perhaps increased cognitive functioning over the more absolute PI level person). But with only a partially functioning ability to think "about," that is, dual-processing representational abilities only primitively or incompletely formed, the internal voice that you and I commonly use and experience would only be poorly managed. Instead of seamless movement between the imagined internal voice and outside expression or management of co-occurring external stimuli, the internal voice may need to "be made" external. As a result, the songs, sounds, and statements that we can imagine on our second layer of processing tracks can't be consistently managed, and by necessity, internal becomes external in the child with autism. Given persistent focus on parts and a preference for constancy, the internal "clip" would be expressed externally in a repeated and almost obsessional manner.

Another common symptom of autism that was mentioned earlier is behavior problems such as tantrums, aggression, and self-injurious behavior (SIB). The object-based preference for constancy is likely central to much of this behavior, but we can use other parts of the theory to better understand why these types of behaviors make sense for the child with autism. Recall once again our robot example: If you preferred things in a certain way and these robot machines around you were somehow related to making things happen according to your preferences but now were not doing so, wouldn't you have a tantrum? Now add to this equation an inability to understand the robot as a whole unit and an inability to communicate with the robot—there is really not much left to do but have a tantrum. You might even lash out at this irritating and uncooperative machine, and if that worked to correct the situation, associative learning would lead you to repeat the behavior. Similarly, SIB makes sense if you imagine parts of your body as disconnected things that are always nearby. For example, I chew on my pen-top when I work. This is a disconnected thing that is pretty continually nearby, but granted, it does not hurt as much as if I did the same thing to my finger. But remember, there is no unified, whole "me" in the child with severe autism, so hitting, biting, or picking at his or her body or otherwise doing those things that hurt would not really matter as much. The connection between body parts and "me" does not exist anymore than chewing my pen-top hurts me. As a side note, the absence of the symbol-based "me" suggests a more object-based identification; consistent with this theory, SIB behaviors should be more prevalent at the PI or EH levels, as compared to IH or WH.

For reasons similar to those surrounding SIB, the common symptom of unusual sensory responsivity also begins to make more and more sense. For the child with autism, incoming sensory stimulation would seemingly come from nowhere, which would be as unusual at it is unsettling. This is difficult for you or I to imagine because we objectively understand what our senses do, that they are an integrated part of what makes up the whole self. But imagine if that were not the case; imagine if every smell, sound, and touch had an undifferentiated, curious, unknowable, stimulatory effect that made no sense at all. It was only registered, much like sensing someone grab your leg, not being sure if it was your leg or your arm, and no one actually being there to do the grabbing. Beyond surprising, this would be confusing and again, potentially terrifying. As a general rule, one can imagine how this situation fuels the likely preference for a quiet, consistent environment for the child with autism.

Similar to this outcome is the person with autism's

tendency toward unregulated mood. Using our theory, I would suggest that mood would be regulated to the extent that the person inherited an evenness of mood; it is only with the ability to self-reflect, self-observe, and control our own reflective cognitive states that mood regulation can be voluntarily achieved. These types of abilities would only become available to the person at the IH and WH levels of identification, although there are exceptions based again on the associative learning model. Cautela and Groden (1978) for example have trained progressive relaxation, which is an example of regulation of one's internal mood state, using basic learning principles of repetition, modeling, and reinforcement.

How does what we've learned apply to treatment?

The continuum-based, dual concepts of inanimate object to whole human object and part-object to whole-object can not only lead to hypothesize developmental effects and groupings, but they can help to explain some of the characteristics of autism that would otherwise appear divergent. It's important to make clear that I believe that the onus of placement or movement on this proposed continuum is predominantly derived from the infant's inherited preferences and predispositions for inanimate object versus human identification. It likely has little to do with the skills or behaviors of the parent, and would not be considered a voluntary choice made by the infant. That is not to say that environment does not play a role or that early, targeted treatment would not be effective. But unlike the original psychoanalytic attempt to explain autism that unfairly and incorrectly blamed the parent, what the child brings to the equation may be most determining of the outcome. This perspective is not new to the psychoanalytic field, as reflected in a quotation from Blanck and Blanck (1986) in my 2011 article:

"Without this capacity on the part of the infant (merger with the parent), the mother's exertions are of little avail. Some

121

infants, with unusual effort on the part of the mother, can be helped to extract somewhat, but principally it is the child who must play his or her part in using what the environment has to offer." (p.15)

I would suggest that it is the interaction of the infant's biological predisposition towards object or human identification, that can be impacted to a degree by the external environment that determines the various trajectories we call autism spectrum disorders. To better understand the relationship between these factors, consider this graphic representation from our 2011 article (Woodard and Van Reet, 2011, p.223; used with permission, Springer Publishing):

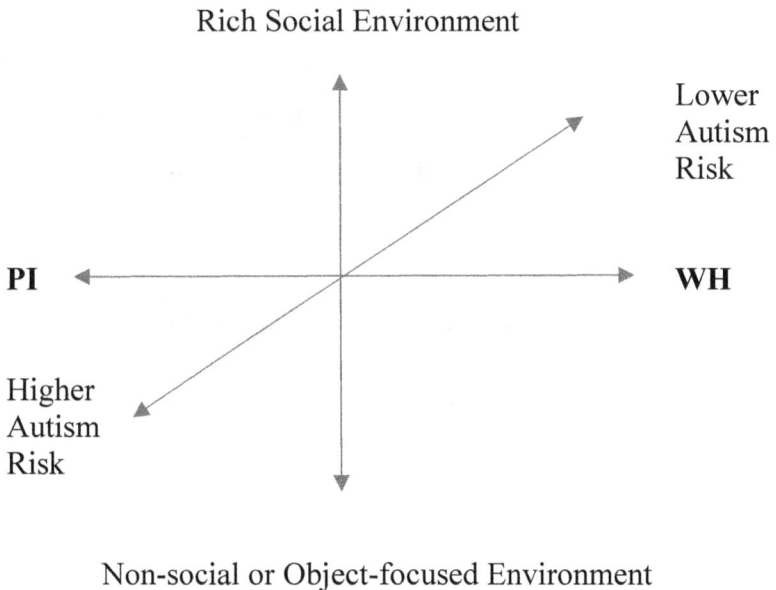

Rich Social Environment

Lower Autism Risk

PI ⟵—————————————⟶ **WH**

Higher Autism Risk

Non-social or Object-focused Environment

Most but not all children typically identify early with human objects with ease and as a result, quickly achieve what we understand to be mature human thinking represented by the ability to think "about." This ultimately allows, at its most complex level, skills far beyond physical object knowledge/problem-solving or understanding the simple intent of others; it allows understanding of even the most subtle social cues and facial expressions, complex person-based problem-solving, multi-faceted self-understanding and self-reflection, acute feelings of empathy and emotional alignment with others, and insight. I would suggest that a small, but apparently expanding group does not identify with human objects and to the extent that they don't, autism emerges. In short:

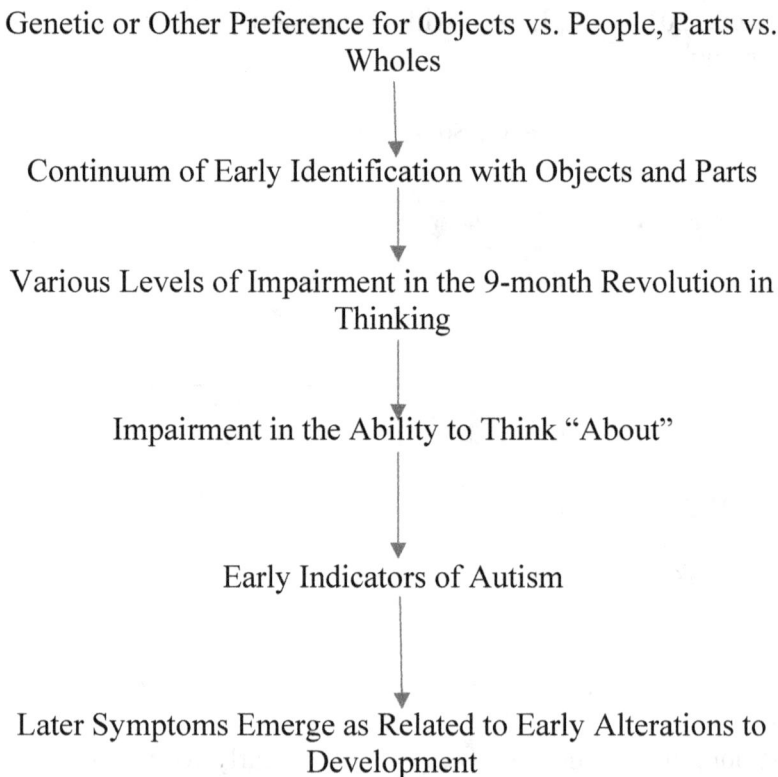

Genetic or Other Preference for Objects vs. People, Parts vs. Wholes

↓

Continuum of Early Identification with Objects and Parts

↓

Various Levels of Impairment in the 9-month Revolution in Thinking

↓

Impairment in the Ability to Think "About"

↓

Early Indicators of Autism

↓

Later Symptoms Emerge as Related to Early Alterations to Development

Chapter 8: Yes, There Is Research to Support These Ideas!

The title of this chapter provides an answer to a fair enough question, especially given the nature of the myriad of ideas that are essential knowledge if we are to truly understand autism. Out of necessity we have discussed many abstract concepts to try to make sense of a disorder that to date has no reasonable theory as to where it comes from, how it develops, or why we see the variations that we see. Because of this, it only seems natural to ask, "Is there any research that supports these ideas?" I have been thinking about this theory for some time as you might have guessed, and hardly a day goes by that I don't see a piece of research and say to myself (because I am a WH identifier), "Of course that is what happened. It makes perfect sense if you think of autism as a result of inanimate object identification instead of person identification." I have tried to collect some examples here, although as stated earlier, I am often hampered by the participant group being simply diagnosed as "autistic." This is likely not a homogenous group as we have seen, although certain pieces of research identify "high functioning" participants, which can be helpful. When you begin research with groups of people whose autism is all at different degrees of severity, of course your results will be difficult to compare to other research that is doing the same thing.

We have, in the last two chapters, identified the more obvious early behavioral expectations that our theory would predict, and if you recall, early on we cited a number of research articles that identified the exact same behaviors: poor eye-gaze, poor response to play attempts and shared social enjoyment, poor joint attention/showing/pointing, using others as tools, and poor or no response to name. From this stand point, these ideas in theory have the potential to make some sense in terms of explaining autism. We have also discussed how this theory might help to explain both common and not-so-common symptoms, such as impaired language development, pronoun reversal, aggressive and self-injurious behavior, and even echolalia. But is there more? Here I have listed some additional behaviors, events, or outcomes that one would expect based on our theory, and what relevant research has revealed:

1) Based on this theory, we would expect that young infants with autism would be as interested or more interested in objects and object-based behavior compared to people and people-based behavior.
And they are. It is already well-documented that children with autism do not attend to people, lack social reciprocity, and enjoy repetitive play with objects. These are defining symptoms of the disorder. Researchers (Hirstein, W., Iverson, P., & Ramachandran, V. S., 2001) have taken this one step further and measured the autonomic responses (electrodermal skin conductance) of children with autism when presented with a cup versus a person's face, as compared to normal control participants. They found no difference in the autonomic responses of children with autism between the two presentations, although there was a difference for the control group. This suggests that for the children with autism, there is really no difference in terms of internal responsiveness between looking at an object and looking at a person; both are really just objects in the mind of the child with autism. Interestingly, the subjects with autism were divided into non-verbal (27%), some verbal communication (49%), and normal linguistic ability (24%), which are groupings that could correspond somewhat to our PI, EH, and IH levels on the identification continuum. Comparisons by these groupings were not noted in the research, which is unfortunate because our theory would predict increasing

autonomic responsivity for the higher functioning group. However, there is this statement tucked in at the bottom of page 1885 that does point in our expected direction:

> "Interestingly, we also noticed a trend towards above-normal SCRs to locking gaze in our higher functioning subjects, which we are currently testing experimentally."

Further, Klin and his colleagues (Klin et al., 2009) worked with 2 year-olds with autism and found that they failed to orient to point-light displays of biological motion, which are points of light that put together, look like people moving. Instead of engaging in this essential and common behavior, the children with autism looked at non-social, physical contingencies (the same point-light displays inverted and played backwards). Typically developing children did the opposite and oriented to the biological motion as one would expect; an essential behavior not only given the adaptive advantages of being likely to attend to other living things, but also the neural foundation for this behavior overlaps with brain regions involved in perceiving basic social information such as facial expression. Note that this behavior is not only typically present very early in a wide range of species, but also present as early as the first few days of life in human infants. A strong human tendency indeed! The finding that it is not present in young children with autism is significant, and confirms what we have hypothesized, that non-social, object-based patterns are simply more interesting to young children with autism compared to people-based patterns.

Celani (2002) conducted a research project that shows the type of thing we are discussing in about the simplest terms possible. He had three participant groups: 12 with autism, 12 with Down Syndrome, and 12 typically developing children. Each participant in each group had four conditions with various types of preference choices to make: 1) human beings and inanimate objects, 2) animals or inanimate objects, 3) pictures of a child handling an object, and 4) pictures of a child in contact with a human. Only the group of children with autism differed from the other two groups, and only in two conditions: the conditions with people in them. The children with autism consistently preferred the object choice over the people choice. And finally, Bodfish (2011) has suggested that autism is related to activation of the different brain circuitries for social versus non-social reward. For the person with autism, there is under-activation of the social area, and over-activation of the non-social area. As you can see, the evidence is quite clear here and easily collected and interpreted: young children with autism prefer objects over people.

2) Based on this theory, we would expect that no single genetic marker would be evident, but rather that the more common genetic anomalies would map onto areas that could be hypothesized to be related to early, person-based identification. And they are. We know from our earlier discussions that there is no single gene that has been found to be responsible for the emergence of autism. However, genetic anomalies common to some persons with autism have been found, and these anomalies are located where we expect them to be based on our theory: in areas related to how early relationships with others are formed. For example, Ylisaukko-oja et al. (2006) discovered that the best such genetic marker (D3S3691) was near a region of oxytocin-related regulation of human attachment and associated social behaviors. These types of findings have been found time and time again; Chakrabarti el al. (2009) located three autism-related genes in the oxytocin-vasopressin system, including OXTR, OXT, and AVPR1B. These genes are related to the emergence of empathy, prosocial measures, and trust. In a similar vein, Guastella et al. (2008) found that oxytocin levels played a role in gaze specifically toward the eye region of human faces.

This type of research supports the idea that in the search for a gene or set of genes for autism, the most likely culprit will probably be any gene that has the potential to affect the early human identification process: preference for human eye gaze, preference for human or inanimate object orientation, sensitivity to touch, sensitivity to human voices, preference for repeating movement or sound, etc. Based on these traits, I would suggest that there is no "thing" called autism at the beginning, but rather a set of predispositions that, under the right circumstances, affects the developmental course of identification in a manner that results in a variety of traits and behaviors that we have chosen to call autism spectrum disorders.

3) Based on this theory, we would expect that treatment modalities that foster interpersonal engagement early would show an effect, mainly because the adult is inadvertently encouraging movement on our proposed continuum. This is complemented by basic behavioral techniques, the underlying cognitive foundations of which (associative learning and recognition memory) remain accessible to the person with autism.

And they do. In the early chapters of this book, I noted that effective, early interventions were those that employed established behavioral techniques within the framework of a pointed, person-based program. Popular versions of such models include Pivotal Response Training (PRT) and the Denver Model. PRT for example, employs applied behavior analytic (ABA) techniques and focuses on increasing a child's desire to learn skills related to imitation, language, and play. Similarly, the Denver Model employs selected behavioral teaching techniques within the framework of an interpersonal relationship. But as we stated earlier, it is the one-on-one engagement and human interaction that likely forms the centerpiece of many of these effective forms of treatment. No video, no self-management, no toys, no Skinnerian reinforcement machine, and no set of physical surroundings result in the same positive change. It is the involvement or duration of the therapist's presence seems to make the difference between effective and non-effective treatment. At least 15 to 25 hours of intensive treatment (accompanied by trained, parent engagement at other times) is an essential part of making these interventions work. In the next chapter, we will discuss how the present theory could possibly be used to maximize treatment efforts, and potentially focus therapeutic efforts further for even better outcomes.

4) Based on this theory, we would expect that there would be a lessening deficit in symbolic or pretend play as one moved up the proposed continuum.
And there is. While it is often difficult to identify where participants in certain studies might fall on our proposed continuum, research such as Wing et al. (1977) and Mundy et al. (1986) suggested that participants with autism had severely impaired pretend play abilities. These were marked by varying levels of impairment from an absence of pretend play to less spontaneous, complex, and varied (more repetitive) symbolic play as compared to typically developing children. In the Wing et al. research, for example, a total of 56 participants were diagnosed as having "complete" autistic syndrome: simple stereotypies (repetitive, non-purposeful movements) with little or no social contact, no initiation of social contact, repetitive speech, and only two of the 56 showed evidence of symbolic play. Of the 56, 32 showed no play whatsoever, and the remaining participants engaged in stereotypical play only. However, later researchers (Lewis & Boucher, 1995; Charman et al., 1997) found participants with autism who were able to engage in pretend play equal to the

matched control participants. While some of the participants needed to be cued and pressured into engaging in this behavior, more typical symbolic play was present in this group with autism. This research was particularly significant in the field of autism because it supposedly called into question the meta-representational explanation of the disorder. But how can two sets of research result in such different findings? The central difference was that the children with autism who were able to engage in pretend play were "high functioning." This different starting point is exactly what our theory would lead us to expect in terms of results found. Other research that supports the emergence of pretend play in children with autism also notes the role of the highly structured experimental environment, and the general lack of spontaneous play (McDonough et al., 1997).

5) Based on this theory, psychotropic medications designed to help organize thinking and decrease an obsessive need for constancy would be effective.

And they are. Anyone who works with families affected autism has likely been faced at some point or another, with the issue of medication usage. This is a particularly difficult decision, because the parent has already had to struggle with being told that their child has a poorly understood disorder that is lifelong and only moderately responsive to intensive, early treatment. Even with the best behavioral interventions, certain behaviors can persist that are potentially dangerous to either the person with autism or those in his or her environment, and now the parent is being faced with having to discuss medications that are typically used for persons with very severe mental disorders. I have had more than one parent say to me, "So now you are telling me that my child is crazy," or, "Are they going to make them into a zombie?" This process is, of course, difficult for the practitioner as well, but the positive effects that can be derived from responsible medication usage are significant. Still, behavioral psychologists seem to struggle particularly hard with this fact, and at least in my own experience, have often considered medication usage a type of behavioral "cop-out." For the behavioral psychologist, medications seem to be only attempts to "chemically restrain" or sedate, and while not typically stated overtly, there exists the view that medications are the crutch of the behaviorally uninformed and incompetent. Personally, I don't believe this to be true, but there are many differing opinions on medication usage for persons with autism.

To a degree, there is a reason for this type of thinking. Aligned with Bettleheim's incorrect explanation of autism, the history of psychotropic medication usage is unfortunately marred by over-use of a relatively small group of potent and sedating drugs that were accompanied by serious side effects. Such a negative history has been further perpetuated by popular media in films like "One Flew Over the Cuckoo's Nest" and "Beauty and the Beast." But the truth is that responsible medication use has the potential to do a lot of good (Myers, 2007), and when things go very badly, even the most behaviorally oriented practitioner will call upon a psychiatric hospital. Today, 50% to 70% of children diagnosed with autism are on some type of psychotropic medication, and good data that shows a reduction of behavioral challenges and improved accessibility to behavioral interventions are (or at least should be) the measures of success.

Over the past 30 years, the types of psychotropic medications available have expanded dramatically, and while research on their use for persons with autism is only now accumulating, the FDA has approved certain medications for the treatment of behavioral challenges and irritability associated with autism (Myers, 2007). Interestingly, these particular approved medications are technically classified as "anti-psychotics," which is a term that can be distressing for a parent because of the layperson's understanding of the word "psychotic." But they are called this because they are effective for persons who primarily have disordered thinking, and associated mood and behavioral problems. So, certain approved medications that are effective for persons with autism are those that help to organize the central thought processes, by bringing a calming order to chaotic and confusing cognitive processing. These medications are not designed primarily for mood, anxiety, attention disorders, or other mental disorders (although they can help with these issues in certain situations). Rather, they are designed to help organization of thinking and internal regulation. In our theory, the central effect of object identification versus human identification is that very area, because object identification robs the person of the ability to think "about" to varying degrees. Without this ability, thinking can be severely impaired and disordered, and the world is likely experienced as a confusing and stressful place. It should then come as no surprise that this category of medication is particularly effective, and related medications that affect anxiety, obsessive repetition, and mood can also be of help.

6) Based on this theory, infants who are on the developmental trajectory of autism should have unusual eye-gaze behaviors as early as the first birthday, and this should continue through the second year of life. Equal interest in various parts of the face and other objects in the environment should predict autism.

Research in the area of infant gaze is challenging, but we do have some evidence that eye-gaze is abnormal relatively early in life for the child with autism. Clifford and Dissanayake (2008) used retrospective parental interviews and home videos to explore early eye-gaze behavior and behaviors related to early expression of affect during the first two years of life. Thirty-six children with autism were compared to typically developing controls. Anomalies in both eye-gaze and emotional expression were evident as early as

133

6 months, and became more severe as the child progressed towards his or her second birthday. In similar research, Jones, Carr, and Klin (2008) presented 10 videos of someone looking directly at a camera to a group of 2 year-old children with autism. The person on the video was engaging in typical game-like behaviors such as peek-a-boo. Eye tracking measures of the children with autism did not show the typical level of interest in the eyes, common to a typical comparison group and a comparison group with developmental delay but not autism. The group with autism's gaze toward the eyes of the person on the video was significantly less than the other two groups, and looking at the mouth (rather than the eyes) was increased. Further, the less the children with autism fixated on the eyes of the person in the video, the greater that child's level of social disability. In other words, the greater the avoidance of and non-realization of people as special objects with unique and preferred qualities, the greater the degree or severity of the autistic disorder.

7) Based on this theory, we would expect that children with autism would most likely have physical awareness of their object-existence (especially above the PI level).
The crux of our theory is that infants with autism identify primarily at the object/part-object end of an inanimate- to human-object/ part- to whole-object continuum. We suggest that the degree of movement along this continuum, derived from identification, defines how the person perceives the world and the self, primarily as a function of the ability to think "about" or imagine. At the most inanimate object/part-object end of the continuum, we would expect the ability to think "about" or imagine to be most impaired, and associated with a desire for physical object constancy, which would be supported by only recognition-based memory skills in contrast to recall-based skills. A desire for physical object constancy seems to come dangerously close to the concept of

thinking "about" because knowing that a thing is different suggests simultaneous knowledge of how it should be the same; these concepts are closely related to research in autism on object permanence and visual self-recognition. As noted earlier, one would think that the skill of object permanence should only be present above the PI level, yet it also occurs prior to the behaviors that are representative of the 9-month revolution for typically developing children.

Object constancy, object permanence, and physical self-recognition could potentially go a number of ways in terms of our theory. Are these unique core elements of even the PI level of identification? Do they emerge separate from other thinking "about" abilities? Or are they thinking "about" abilities that correspond to our levels of identification? Another option to these being a function of a single thinking "about" skill would be that the ability to think "about" emerges in an increasingly complex progression. For example, the ability to think about an object continuing to exist where it was last seen would seem most basic. Next, knowing that the object continued to exist but was moved to another location, or all objects being in a certain order, would be more sophisticated. Understanding that the object changed its form somehow but was still the same object would be still more complex—and these types of rules could extend to people, such as wanting a person to physically always look the same or say the same thing.

It is currently unclear how our theory of identification would necessarily play out in this particular set of circumstances, given all of these possibilities, the comparatively early emergence of object permanence in typical development, and the unique role of objects in our theory. One likely possibility is that children on the developmental trajectory of autism may have difficulty in these areas at the most severe PI level, but beyond that level would have knowledge of the self as a physical object much as they recognize

135

other physical objects. Research in the 1980s found that children with autism who were not severely cognitively impaired would remove a mark from their faces when they saw the mark on their face in a mirror image (Dawson & McKissick, 1985), but the experimental group of 15 children had intellectual functioning ranging from a severe deficit (IQ = 17) to nearly normal functioning (IQ = 89). This variation within an experimental group makes it difficult to draw conclusions from the results in relation to the present theory. Further research in this area is clearly needed and would provide insights into this complex area.

8) Based on this theory, there should be some improvement in the comprehension or functioning of concepts that require a person to think "about," such as past and present, what "could" happen (and related or resulting fear response), death, hypothetical problem-solving, or even lying, as one moved up the proposed continuum.

Again, we are faced with the problem that most research does not divide participants into groups that would correspond with our continuum demarcations. However, there is research that begins to support these ideas. The area of thinking about past and present, for example, has been explored by Lind and Bowler (2010), but this is one of only a handful of research projects addressing these particular concepts. These researchers used high-functioning participants with autism (who would correspond roughly to the IH level on our continuum), and found that participants with autism "recalled/imagined" significantly fewer events than typical control participants, and episodic future memory was also impaired as compared to controls. These findings are consistent with our current theory in that at the IH level, as a result of increasingly human object identification, these "high-functioning" persons with autism can access impaired thinking "about" abilities. Interestingly, the participants with autism were more likely to take a third-person versus a first-person perspective in recalling events, which highlights the associated impaired concepts of self that would continue to plague the person at the IH level.

Similarly, high-functioning persons with autism have shown abnormal (or impaired but not absent) acquisition of a fear response (Gaigg & Bowler, 2007). For example, at the center where I work, we have a yearly Halloween party. One year I thought it would be fun for the children to make a hole in the wall, surrounded by a skull and a sign that read, "Put your hand in if you dare!" This turned out to be of virtually no interest to our students who all have severe presentations of autism; each one stuck his or her hand in the hole without any concern at all, took the candy offered, and left. There was absolutely no concern over what might happen if they put their hand in the hole. Along the same lines of thinking, preschool children with autism who had average intellectual functioning and vocabulary skills were able to provide alternatives to social problems (Bernard-Opitz, Sriram, & Nakhoda-Sapuan, 2001), although they produced significantly fewer alternatives compared to control participants as we would expect. However, they were able to improve upon this skill across probes, which we would also expect given their higher functioning thinking "about" capacities. Finally, while research is virtually non-existent on autism and the concept of death, the problem of persons with autism in understanding death and understandably responding in the expected unusual ways, has been addressed (Forrester-Jones & Broadhurst, 2007). The concept of being and then not being is a very difficult one for persons on the spectrum. Taken as a whole (there is no known research on autism and the ability to tell a lie), these supposedly differing areas of research converge on one idea: emerging applied skills and concepts appear as one's thinking "about" capacities improve.

9) Others should be treated as mechanical tools and there should be more interest in parts of objects as compared to whole objects, again, to a lessening degree as one moved up the continuum.

Research specifically addressing the level of autism and others being treated as tools has not been conducted to my knowledge. However, using other people's bodies to communicate (usually by placement of another person's hand on an object without a coordinated gaze with that person's eyes) is a key diagnostic component of the Autism Diagnostic Observation Schedule (ADOS; Lord, Rutter, DiLavore, & Risi, 2002). This test is the "gold-standard" currently used for the diagnosis of autism. According to ADOS, using another person's body as a tool is not only one of the important coding items for autism, but it is one of the five scored coding items, meaning that it feeds directly into the cut-off score for the "Communication Total" to diagnose autism. Clearly, perceiving others as objects to be used is a central marker of autism.

Similarly, one of the diagnostic sections of the ADOS scoring rubric is "Unusually Repetitive Interests or Stereotyped Behaviors." This section includes any preoccupation with objects, repetitive use of toys, repetitive actions, and insistence on routines. But when we look closer, the example for pre-occupation with objects includes "table legs" and "wrist watches;" not tables and arms of people with watches on them, but just the legs and the watch. To make this clearer, the scoring description for this section specifically states, "a clear interest in a part of an object." A number of studies (Liss et al., 2006; Mann & Walker, 2003) have indirectly addressed this area, mainly through researching what are known as "attentional abnormalities." In Liss et al. for example, 144 persons with autism were rated on a number of scales measuring attentional and sensory focus. What these researchers found through cluster analysis was that there was the expected over-focused pattern of attention in nearly half of the participants. This intensive over-selection of parts of objects was thus suggested to be a prime symptom of autism, and the authors review a range of possible neurological correlates.

10) Based on this theory, persons with a known, inherited object focus would have a greater likelihood of developing autism.

It is generally accepted that females are, as a group only and with many individual exceptions, superior to males in language abilities, perceptual speed, and verbal memory, and that females have faster language acquisition. Females have even been found to be more interested in facial than spatial or mechanical stimuli as early as birth (Knickmeyer & Baron-Cohen, 2006). Males, on the other hand, as a group again with many exceptions, are superior in mental rotation skills, motor abilities, and spatial perception. While the literature on gender-based cognitive differences shows great variability across studies, these findings alone would lend themselves to a male predisposition toward objects.

Baron-Cohen (2002) took this idea one step further when he suggested that autism was the result of an extreme male brain (EMB), or a hyper-male cognitive profile. In the EMB theory, female brains are characterized by a focus on "empathizing," and male brains are characterized by a focus on "systematizing." Empathizing leads one to better understand the emotions of others, while systematizing supports the ability to analyze the variables of a system, which is closely related to skills such as visual-spatial reasoning. Again, with comparatively poorer people-based skills such as empathizing and language acquisition, and comparatively better object-based skills such as mental rotation and figure-disembedding (Falter, Plaisted, & Davis, 2008), if autism results from a tendency to identify with objects, is it really surprising that males with autism outnumber females 4:1? Once again, this is completely consistent with the theory offered here.

11) Based on this theory, if there is any evidence of parent commonalities, they should be in the direction of inanimate object interest and poor social skills. However, given the theorized, comparatively strong role of the infant in creating autism, any parent commonalities should be weak and non-universal.

There is growing evidence that there is a broader autism phenotype in families, which is a complex way of saying that family members of children with autism tend to have more subtle versions of the features of autism. A study by Piven et al. (1997) reviewed research that showed parents of children with autism tended to lack emotional responsiveness, show impaired empathy, and display special interest patterns and odd social communication. This was, of course, not true of all parents of children with autism, but with many. Related research suggested that fathers of children with Asperger's Syndrome tended to show social deficits, and first-degree relatives had significantly higher rates of communication and social deficits, and repetitive behaviors. Piven's research was consistent with past research, and found higher rates of social deficits and stereotyped behaviors in relatives of families with autism as compared to families with a person with Down syndrome. This research supports the idea of poor social skills, but what about object interest? There is no known research addressing this area specifically.

12) Infants who experienced events that similarly affected the identification process should have approximations of autism-related traits and behaviors.

And they do. If we consider the identification process, the infant with an autism trajectory theoretically brings a predisposition for inanimate object focus, which we have suggested is likely the function of genetic origins. Compared to this part of the autism equation, what the environment affects or induces is likely to be relatively small. That is not to say that we can't make a difference and should not try, but rather that given this situation, we need to direct and maximize our environmental impact however possible. Trying to affect the situation from the genetic side (by, for example, discouraging pregnancy for parents with the autism phenotype or one child with autism) would not be appropriate.

So, what environmental factors are involved in the typical identification process? We could hypothesize that emotion- and communication-laden interactions with the infant, eye-gaze, touch, reciprocal social interchanges, more person interactions than object interactions, and the like are probably crucial. If we wanted to inhibit this process in some significant way, we could take eye-sight out of the mix, which would undoubtedly impair much of what is going on in the identification process. If we were to do that, is autism more likely to result? To explore this hypothesis, Brown, Hobson, Lee, and Stevenson (1997) studied children ages 3 to 9 years who had been totally or almost totally blind since birth, and rated them on a standardized autism rating scale. The results showed that 10 of the 24 children assessed met the diagnostic criteria for autism, although these 10 children were not quite the same as a child with autism. Specifically, of the 10 children for whom we assume the blindness "induced" a version of autism, only a small percentage had the same type of emotional and social impairment representative of a truly autistic presentation. However, other traits were present.

13) If a child develops autism as a result of identifying with objects instead of people, not only should they interact with others as if they were objects but their own behavior would be that of a conscious, yet inanimate object.

Recall that in our theory, identification with other people allows us to think "about" in the most sophisticated manner possible, and to comprehend ourselves as people. It would follow then that if we identified instead with objects, we would see the world solely in object form, and conceive of ourselves solely as objects. While this is somewhat difficult to imagine, try to think of yourself as a thing only, with only biologically induced emotional states. If you were a conscious and mobile inanimate object as we are suggesting, how would you behave? This turns out to be a very difficult thing for even the most sophisticated thinkers to do. We have already suggested that there would be little, if any fear of what might happen. Therefore, without supervision, the person with this thinking perspective would not likely avoid danger for very long. Further, not being able to understand the self as a connected whole makes self-injurious behaviors almost reasonable. But if we consider what we typically do to objects, a ball for example, we could hypothesize even further: we might slap it, bite it, throw it, bounce it, spin it, squeeze it, shake it, roll it, or otherwise simply handle it. For the person reading this who works with people with autism, you are most likely saying to yourself, "Hmmm. Those are things I see in children with autism all the time." I can't tell you how many times I have seen a child with autism throw themselves on the floor or against a wall completely without reason or warning, or how many times I have had a student ask me for "squeezes." Children with autism commonly bite themselves, spin, roll, and love to wrap themselves in "body socks," "squeeze machines," and use weighted vests and blankets. We have all sorts of occupational therapy-based, internal regulation theories trying to explain why this happens, but isn't it simpler to suppose that this person perceives himself or herself as an object and is simply acting accordingly?

Chapter 9: How Technology May Be at the Root of Autism

Let's take a moment to summarize what we have discussed up to this point. I have suggested that, for some reason we have yet to discuss, infants are being born with a genetic predisposition to prefer inanimate objects and "parts," over people and "wholes." The strength of this predisposition can vary significantly from infant to infant, putting the onus of autism development strongly in this hypothesized area of the genetic realm. Not that there is nothing we can do to alter the emergence of autism, but that this predisposition plays a very significant role. This means that when it is time to take part in a developmental cognitive shift around age 1 to 2 years that requires interest in humans for identification, these toddlers identify instead (to varying degrees) with their preferred inanimate objects. This in turn, impairs the cognitive shift that is marked by the ability to meta-represent or "think about," and what we know as autism emerges. This identification impairment happens on a continuum of severity, causing a range or "spectrum" of presentations. There are early markers that this theory explains, and it also explains how new, previously curious and apparently unrelated symptoms emerge as the child ages. This theory also explains why autism emerges around age 2, and suggests that all symptoms across the lifespan can be traced back to this core impaired ability to "think about." Not only does this explanation make good sense, I have shown you research study after research study that supports these ideas.

The next question that you may ask is, if we have increasing rates of autism, why are more and more children being born with this supposed predisposition toward inanimate objects? The answer I would suggest is that this growing predisposition is the result of years and years of a growing cultural preoccupation with objects. When my parents were younger, they engaged almost all the time with other people, and spent comparatively less time with things. They played together, ate together, communicated directly person to person, and had much more social and personal and human interaction than we do today. Over the years, technology introduced things that drew this human attention and interaction rate down steadily, year by year and decade by decade. Although no one has really measured this decline, think about it. First there was the influence of radio. When you see pictures of families "enjoying" the radio, what do you see? A group of people not talking to each other, typically looking around at different places in the room. It is actually a bit uncomfortable, much like playing a song for someone or a recording; there is nothing to look at because you are just listening to something and yet you don't want to just stare at the other person, so you find something else to look at. After radio came the advent of television, where not only did people stop talking with each other, they began looking at an object for hours on end. Human interaction rates further diminished, and what increased was our fascination with this box that delivered so much entertainment and enjoyment. Fortunately, much of what was presented on television included people, so when you think of our theory of how autism develops and the diminishing person to person contact in the mid-20th century, the effects may have been mitigated somewhat.

After television what happened next may have been the proverbial nail in the coffin of social interaction: the introduction and proliferation of the computer, internet, video games, and now the "smart" phone. Year after year, since the 1950s, we as a society have increased our time spent interacting with objects and decreased our time interacting with each other. Currently the average millennial or generation Xer spends a whopping 3 to 4 hours online per day—and some people even sleep with their phones. All of this screen time is at the expense of person-to-person interaction, and undoubtedly parent-to-child interaction (although some people consider shared media events like gaming a form of "interaction"). It really shouldn't surprise anyone that research on adolescents, young adults, and adults over the past 2 decades shows media exposure increases from year to year; all you need to do is do a quick search on the internet to see what firms that are interested in this area have found.

Or perhaps you want to go way back and see how TV watching habits have changed since 1950. Feel free to look this up as well on the internet, but what you will find is an ever-increasing number of hours watching TV from the 1950s to the present day. Three hours per day, then four, then five—continually staring at a box. It does not really matter where you look or what metric you use to come to the conclusion that western culture and modern society—those of most developed countries—have slowly and consistently redirected our focus toward objects and away from people and each other. I have no source for showing you a graph of how social interaction has decreased since 1950 or how focus on objects has increased, because no one really measures that. But it is so apparent what has happened, that I don't even think one is needed.

We become that with which we identify

It is nearly impossible to turn in any direction without finding evidence of increased cultural object focusing. On a flight, for example, someone across the aisle was reading a newspaper article titled something like, "Up to 8 Hours: A Harmless Distraction?" The article was about how, on average, people now spend up to 8 hours each day engaged with a phone, computer, video-game or other "thing" at the expense of human interaction or just sitting and thinking. If we consider the possible effect of this amount of screen time on one's ability to do their part in the process of identification, is it really harmless? The article mainly discussed the potentially negative effects that too much screen time might be having on the cognitive development of the current and next generation. But I could not help but think about our theory and consider the implications of an entire culture being trained to engage with objects for increasing amounts of time on a continual basis. Based on the theory I have put forth, one hypothetical way to increase the prevalence of autism would be to have culture-wide focusing away from people and towards objects, impairing the population's people-focusing and human interaction skills, and/or perhaps subsequently, impairing their ability to foster human identification in their children. Not only may the quality of interactions with children change, but the sheer time spent engaged in this essential process may be lessened. When the person reading the paper turned to me and said, "Before you know it, we will all be computers!" I smiled back and nodded my head, and thought to myself that this was exactly the implication: we become that with which we identify. What's more, consider each time you turn on the TV and there is a commercial about how technological gadgets are all-consuming. It makes for a funny commercial to see people staring at their phones and walking out in front of moving cars as a result, but when you consider where we have hypothesized that autism comes from, is this really something we should find amusing?

One of the most disturbing manifestations of this phenomenon that I encounter is when I see two people out to dinner or on a walk. These people should be talking to or looking at each other, but instead they are texting, checking messages, or otherwise interacting with their devices instead. Sometimes this is a couple for whom I wonder if this was all they had hoped their first date to be, but sometimes it is a parent and child. The parent is engaged with their object of choice, while the child wanders about, looking for something to interact with—or even worse, the child is also using an electronic device. I wonder how much this happened during the first year of development, and what effect this type of culture-wide interaction (or lack thereof) has on this child learning to do the same. Will they find some other thing on which to focus? If they do, will this person as an adult become unconsciously attracted to someone who similarly prefers to look at and interact with objects instead of each other? What are the genetics of these two combined, object-focused people, and what kind of genetic predisposition might they produce when they have a child? When they do produce someone, how likely are they to look at or interact with the child? Or will they be so busy checking their newest gadget that the child will really become more of an interruption?

It is not news that emailing and texting has become nearly an addiction. Phyllis Hanlon (2010) reported that the BBC had run a story about two adolescents undergoing treatment for cell phone addiction, and discussed whether or not such a classification as a disorder was truly warranted. But more importantly, she added that one-half of all U.S. teens send more than 100 texts per day and 87% sleep with or near their phone. But haven't teens always spent a lot of time on the phone? The answer to this is likely to be a resounding "yes," but what is the effect of non-voice and non-personal interaction at this rate, combined with all the other lost human interaction that at one time routinely happened in our culture? What does this type of experience mean for our ability to read the human cues of others? What does it do to our desire to engage the gaze of an infant?

Taking cultural cues: what it means that anorexia and autism have a lot in common

The answers to these questions are not simple ones, but the suggestion that a cultural phenomenon could worsen or even produce a psychological disorder over time, to the extent that the disorder starts to run in families and is now "heritable" is not a new or unique idea. Consider the psychological disorder known as anorexia, which is an eating disorder where the person restricts his or her intake of food and becomes excessively thin. It is related to and sometimes accompanied by bulimia, where the person, in addition to restricting food intake, binges and purges. The complications that can result from this disorder, as you can imagine are severe, and include all sorts of issues with the heart, blood pressure, malnutrition, bone development, female reproduction, and many others. The death and suicide rates associated with anorexia are significant. There are often associated symptoms of depression, anxiety, inaccurate perception of what an appropriate weight may be, issues of control and fear, and sometimes self-harm. It is sometimes said to be more common in people for whom appearance is important or essential (models or actors, for example). It typically affects females more often, with the female to male proportion reported as about 9:1, and the prevalence rate is about 8 per 100,000 people (Hoek, 2006). Anorexia rates increased in past decades most significantly in females age 15-24, and is more common in white females than black females. The prevalence rate among females ranges, depending on what you are measuring, from about 0.3% to 1%.

The first thing that is evident about anorexia is that much like autism is seen predominantly in males, anorexia is seen predominantly in females. Now let's turn to look at theories about where anorexia comes from, although you might be able to guess what is coming next. There are a number of ideas on this topic, but generally anorexia is explained to be the result of a complex combination of biological and environmental factors, the exact cause of which is not known. It is a significantly heritable disorder with heritability rates between 28% and 58% (Thorton, 2011). Building on the genetic prevalence information we discussed earlier, I will note that heritability rates are 53% for dizygotic

149

twins for autism, and higher for monozygotic twins (Tick et al., 2016). Multiple genes have been shown to influence or be related to the emergence of this disorder, but no single gene has been found to be responsible. And these genes do not explain by any means, all of the cases of anorexia that are seen. Sounding familiar?

In terms of the environmental causes, this disorder is most prevalent in societies or cultures where thinness is valued, and the thin person is the ideal or "perfect" body type. So there is more of it where a certain cultural idea is more prevalent. This is communicated in various ways through all sorts of social media, newspapers, magazines, TV, and the internet. In addition to these cultural influences, if the person is under constant pressure early in life to be thin, or has had some type of early trauma, some researchers believe these factors can contribute to the emergence of the disorder. Not surprisingly, personality traits for persons with this disorder tend to be marked by core feelings of loss of control, inadequacy, and low self-esteem, as well as difficulty maintaining good relationships with others. The anorexic individual tends to be a high achiever—even a perfectionist—longing to be the happy, ideal person that might evolve, if only (as the associated thinking pattern goes) he or she were thinner.

So like autism, anorexia is more common in one gender, has a significant heritable component, and genes do not explain the whole picture. Most interestingly, anorexia, much like autism, was something typically not seen in the early 1900s. That is not to say that it didn't exist; there are case studies dating back to the 1800s. But it was not until the 1950s and into the 1970s that the incidence rate picked up considerably. If you simply look at the number of studies that have been done since that time (a good indicator of the prevalence of a disorder), what you will find is increasing rates from about 100 per year in 1970, to around 300 per year in the '80s and '90s, to over 500 studies in 2012.

Notice that this trend suggests that as the root causes of the disorder are becoming more pervasive in a culture, there is a leveled off period, and then around 1982, the real increase begins. Today, about 8 million people in the United States are estimated to have anorexia or a related eating disorder, almost double what it was in the mid 1900s. That's about 2% of the population, or 1 in every 50 people. How could this happen? If you have a cultural, shared experience where strong messages are being delivered to a population, and you start early enough and affect development, those messages can result in lifelong problems that are difficult to correct. Interestingly, there is also a continuum of severity of anorexia, and while it is seen as a lifetime disorder, recovery is often noted to be on a "spectrum" of quite good to poor. If people who have this disorder increase in a population and then have children, the predisposition for certain personality traits are passed down. This "heritable component" in anorexia may create or be a predisposition that prepares the infant or child to interpret or perceive the world around him or her in a certain way, making him or her more vulnerable to certain environmental conditions. As the messages continue throughout the culture and become more and more embedded, the incidence rate rises over time. If left untreated or unchecked, the prevalence of the disorder will continue to increase. Fortunately, in the case of anorexia, this happened less due to increased awareness and good, targeted treatment becoming available.

Similar to what we have previously suggested for autism, a culture, society, or environment where certain conditions are present promotes the production of infants that are at higher risk to be vulnerable to the effects of these conditions. As those certain cultural or societal conditions remain in effect or become more pervasive, a kind of feedback loop is created where, left untreated, the disorder becomes more prevalent.

It's no wonder autism is so dramatically on the rise

As you might expect, given this information, it is now not surprising that the incidence of autism has increased from 1 in 2500 in 1985 to 1 in 68 in 2014. Graphs show an early leveled off period from about 1975 to 1985, and then the continual increase begins. Note that anorexia is much more common in western cultures; in less developed countries, typically all that is seen are case reports or very low rates of the disorder. Since we are saying that the effects of less social interaction due to technology may be contributing to the prevalence of autism, you might expect that rates of autism are lower in less developed countries. That is a logical supposition on the surface, but really what we would expect is that the rate of autism would be proportional to the cumulative effects of focus on any object. This would include TVs, phones, and the like. There are very few places where these objects are not present in the world, and even if you could find them, accurate identification of autism is challenging due to the complex nature of the disorder, and data collection as a whole is poor in these less developed countries. It is very challenging to know the actual prevalence of autism around the world, but if we could get an accurate count, this perspective would suggest that to the extent we can estimate the proportion of person-to-person direct interaction as decreasing, that is where autism should, over time, be increasing.

No one single factor causes autism, but...

Before we continue, let me again be perfectly clear: Autism has a strong genetic component, and there is certainly more to the development of autism than a cultural phenomenon where people happen to be looking more and more at objects. I am not suggesting that this phenomenon is the absolute cause of autism, but I am suggesting that: 1) It might be more effective and productive to shift our focus toward genes that may be related to the identification process (or objects versus human identification), and 2) We may be able to produce more effective treatments if we focus on any and every environmental factor that could affect movement toward the human end of the identification continuum we have hypothesized. Just like there are likely to be many genes related to identification in this manner, there are likely to be many environmental factors as well. What is most important is that we start looking for the genes and environmental factors with this theoretical framework (or *a* theoretical framework) in mind. Without a comprehensive theory, we are really just looking everywhere and anywhere without any hint of direction. With that having been said, we can now return to our hypothetical discussion of technology-induced object focus as one possible contributing environmental factor, and then discuss what this all means for the future.

If we allow ourselves to view this as one contributing possibility, we have a singular example of how our theory directs us toward locating other possible reasons for the increase in autism. Consider this "hypothetical" situation: Millions upon millions of people within a culture are spending more and more time *not* engaged with people. Instead, for one reason or another, they are looking at things: computers, phones, or other gadgets, but not people. These gadgets are so consuming and reinforcing that the people in the culture really can't get enough of them. The more the people use them, the more entertaining, need-satisfying, and complex they become, to the point that some call them almost addictive. Because the objects are communication-able and full of information, the people in the culture even put them in their homes, so in addition to carrying around mobile versions and using the same thing at work, these addictive objects are really accessible at all times and in all locations. As more and more time is spent on the objects, proportionately less time is spent interacting with actual people. Further, this electronic connectedness allows and even encourages the socially challenged to enter the fray and become a part of a culture that previously was not particularly available. With the need for actual human interaction eliminated, anyone can become a player at least electronically, and what is created is a culture that is more comfortable with and interested in *things* than they are with people.

Add to this hypothetical phenomenon that half of the culture (the males, let's say) happens to be already genetically more adept at object-based interactions as compared to person-based, so they (as a general group with many exceptions) excel in areas such as spatial skills and object rotation. Further, the use of many of these objects actually improves these very same skills, and more of the group that was genetically geared toward them engages with the objects more than the other part of the larger cultural group (Terlecki & Newcombe, 2005). Not surprisingly, over time, a disorder marked by a preoccupation with objects and a lack of social skill becomes increasingly more and more prevalent within that culture. This disorder is of unknown origins and was at one time rarely identified or diagnosed. Not surprisingly, the group that was noted to be genetically predisposed to objects is also proportionately over-represented in the diagnostic category. Hypothetically, the culture would likely be naturally concerned with this course of events, so to compensate and correct what is happening, multiple attempts might made at rectifying the situation. Because the source of the problem is not clearly understood, researchers in the culture search everywhere for causes and try many different interventions. The only intervention that shows any significant level of effectiveness is typically developing adults spending many, many hours per week promoting person-to-person communication and engagement with the affected child early in development. Still, the cause of the problem evades researchers, and they ask, "What early event or process could be affected in such a way that a seemingly unrelated set of cognitive, social, communicative, and imagination-based skills are impaired to varying degrees? And, why is the nearly forced, intensive interaction with humans the only thing that helps?" I describe this as a hypothetical situation, but it begins to sound all too real.

Chapter 10: Treatment Ideas and Implications for Society

Once you get the idea of how all this might be fitting together, it's difficult not to consider possible interventions, or to interpret new research, behavioral issues, or even current events without considering it. For example, I began to wonder if we could re-initiate some version of the identification process to jump-start movement toward the whole-human end of the continuum and many new questions emerged:

- If we can move toward the whole-human end of the continuum, does it have to happen at the infant/toddler stage, or could we make any progress in ameliorating primary symptoms by intervening when the child is school-age or even an adolescent?
- Is it possible to basically change the infant's mind about humans versus objects and act to shift interest back to the human end of the continuum? Or, if the child comes into the world preferring objects, is that the end of the line?
- Do we need to desensitize young children to humans, or simply reinforce early markers or indicators of human identification?
- Are we really doing the right thing by starting intervention focusing on the behaviors such as poor joint attention and reduced eye gaze to others, or are these truly already symptoms of a more important and earlier identification event?

- What does all of this mean for the young person or young adult at the high end of the ASD spectrum seeking out therapy for social challenges and difficultly engaging with others? What is the core deficit for this person and how might we help with these ideas in mind?
- In the research realm, does this or that article show some intact, yet still impaired ability for the "high-functioning" to think "about"? What does the article mention about a preference for objects, or behavior that could be interpreted as that of a mobile object?
- How is any behavior at any age representative of thinking "about" abilities?
- When staff talk with me about behavioral issues, does it help to understand why someone might be smiling at you while they spit at you if you consider the absence of "other" and the absence of "self"?
- How does the self-as-object reframe the presenting of any behavioral challenge?
- Can we understand it differently or perhaps more as a behavior and less as a personal affront or attack? Does this perspective change what we do… or could do?

There are some very definite things that we can do to address some these concerns, which I will discuss below. But in addition to altering how we intervene to alter the trajectory of any developing autism disorder, I would suggest that if we don't make some significant changes to how we interact and function as a society, autism could continue to increase for years to come. First of all, we need an intervention based on these ideas that works for toddlers that are diagnosed early, and this intervention needs to be implemented across all environments and throughout the child's day. Rather than treating symptoms that are subsequent to an object identification, treatment would be effective to the extent that identification is shifted away from inanimate objects and towards human-based objects. We already know that when children with autism spend large amounts of time with typically developed adults who are specially trained to elicit social interactions and responses, it can have a positive and beneficial effect; we just are not sure why this is the case. This book has explained in detail why this happens. But how can we take our intervention practice even further and refine what happens during the therapeutic hour for the child with autism? If the theory is correct, certain other interventions that shift the identification focus, used in conjunction with proven applied behavioral analysis (ABA) principles, should be effective in improving not only the severity of the symptoms, but the actual core areas of diagnostic impairment. These areas would be most evident on gold-standard tests that indicate the presence of autism early, such as the previously discussed Autism Diagnostic Observation Schedule (ADOS).

Intervention categories for autism

Prior to starting any treatment, our theory suggests that parent training and understanding of the ideas outlined in this book are essential for progress to occur. Before someone can change their behavior even slightly, they need to understand the nature of the desired change and why they are doing what they are doing. To further complicate matters, the necessary interactions may call upon the parent to be more intrusive, forceful, and socially adept than perhaps they prefer to be or perceive themselves as able to be. In addition to parent training, the child needs to be assessed to the extent possible on the more obvious possible sources of non-human preference or human aversion. Is it simply that the child likes objects better, or is there something actually aversive about the voice, touch, eyes, unpredictability, or movement of the human object? Autonomic measures during exposure to these various stimuli might prove helpful, with both over-sensitive and under-sensitive responses helping to guide further treatment and intervention options. Using our more encompassing theoretical orientation and what we already know about autism and effective treatment, any intervention that falls under one of the following main categories might prove helpful in decreasing the core features of autism:

a) **Shifting interest and identification from objects to humans:** Interventions need to be developed that spark and interest in the infant to move along this continuum, and become interested or even unified (to the degree possible) with humans instead of objects. The infant would need to be "met" where they are on this continuum, and then slowly shaped in the desired direction. This component must be embedded in a wide range of activities from the other categories listed, and would be represented in activities such as the presentation of videos that depict first objects, then objects with human emotions or traits, then humans with object traits. Expanding on this idea, any activity that suggests or promotes the changing intent and interest of humans (in contrast to the constancy of objects) would fall under this category.

b) **Shifting conceptualization from part to whole "putting together":** Our theory suggests that not only does the infant with autism need to move from object to human identification, but he or she also needs to put together the parts of things and create whole understanding and conceptualizations. Interventions related to this idea would revolve around literally putting pieces together beginning with objects, then moving on to approximations of people (Mr. Potato

Head, animal toys, and then human dolls). So not only do we incorporate the idea of part moving to whole, but we add in and combine this idea with the shift from object (which is less aversive at the beginning of treatment) to human.

c) **Fostering any "thinking about," representational or imaginative capacity that derives from (a) and (b), preferably from object to human:** The categories above are suggested by our theory to be intricately entwined with this ability. Addressing all of these areas in conjunction with each other may prove to be most helpful. Interventions in this category would first, for example, pair object to object and then pair object to increasingly abstract conceptualizations of this "real" object. In a related way, promoting the infant to imagine the existence of items (and then people as in (a) above) not seen would fall under this category. Interventions that prompt the infant to imagine the intent of another, see a matching substitute of the self, or engage with object-to-human puppets (for example) would fall under this category.

d) **Fostering or reinforcing tolerance of the unpredictability of humans versus the predictability of objects:** As we have discussed, children and persons with autism generally dislike change, prefer routines, and often have difficulty with flexibility and when things do not go as expected. This however, is a common part of life, and the more common, the more one interacts with people; hence one source of anxiety for persons with autism, originating from the identification with objects that are nearly completely predictable in what they do and don't do. People, as you may have noticed, are much less predictable!

Interventions in this category would include objects that operate in first predictable, and second, less predictable ways. Predictable objects are easy to find, but there are unpredictable objects if you search for them, such as a ball with an off-centered weight. It will not roll forward in the manner it should, and can't really be fully predicted. Remote-control toys, operated by another person also fall into this category.

e) **Employing proven ABA techniques:** We already know that these therapies work, so why not use them and integrate them into interventions derived from the categories listed above? The savvy parent, practitioner, or researcher will have already noted the presence of basic ABA principles noted in the categories above. For example, if we want a certain behavior to take place, it is unlikely that we will quickly get the desired end-result behavior right away (especially with an infant). Instead, we will need to meet the infant where he or she is and shape the behavior by breaking the behavior down into steps (task analysis), and then reinforcing (or rewarding) successive approximations of the desired behavior. Reinforcement of these approximations, appropriate and planned prompting techniques, and employing effective strategies such as discrete trial would all be examples of integrating known and effective principles of ABA.

Based on my own research since 2011, I have concluded that it is possible to create interventions derived from these categories. Such interventions in the research we have completed to the present date have shown distinctly positive effects. However, further research would be needed to determine how effective they are in larger group studies. To empirically validate the efficacy of these interventions is an essential step that could take many years to complete, so we have moved forward in developing an intervention set.

Where the Meta-play Method comes in
I began my research in 2011 with a research assistant who took a strong interest in this theory. She and I began with a case study determine if: 1) actual interventions could be created based on the theory-derived categories noted above, and 2) they could effectively be implemented by parents who have a young child with autism. We chose to work with a child with severe autism whose family was intact and was likely to become actively engaged in the therapy. For the child referred to us for this purpose, there were two older siblings in the family who were as interested in what we were doing as the parents. So the "dose" of what we were planning to do was going to be high. Note that this study was not designed to determine the efficacy of the identified interventions; we simply needed to determine if we could create interventions, and if they could be implemented with ease by parents and family members. Efficacy is a larger question that can only be answered through years of carefully controlled research. This means that our only initial goal for the Meta-play Method, which is what we decided to call the intervention set that was created, was to see if we could develop play activities for this toddler that he would take an interest in; if a toddler is not interested in something, he or she will not engage. Over time and with important input from this family, we were able to develop play activities based on our theory, that the parents, siblings and young child with autism engaged in every day. I can't say that he enjoyed them; at least not initially.

We did not want to presume that this Meta-play Method was a stand-alone intervention, so we further researched other treatment models that had shown efficacy. One of those models discussed previously was Pivotal Response Treatment (PRT) (Koegel & Koegel, 2006). To understand how the Meta-play Method could interface with PRT, we set about identifying the main ideas of PRT. We found that PRT is based on a set of things we know about autism: the idea is that if one were able to "correct" main (pivotal) set of concerns, other collateral improvements in functioning would emerge. Some of these main concerns included: 1) a lack of motivation to engage in social encounters, 2) minimal social initiations by the child, 3) problems with self-regulation, 4) poor response to multiple cues, and 5) impaired empathy. As both a developmental approach and one that uses the principles and tools of ABA, PRT puts forth an interactional style that is both related to and directed at these areas in an overlapping and integrated way. We will discuss the interventions the Koegels suggest based on these ideas, but first note the basic theoretical difference between the core ideas of PRT and our theory. By the way, we needed to name out theory, so we decided on the Dynamic Behavior Theory of Autism, or DBT-A. This name comes from the idea that the identification process is a dynamic one; as in the term "psychodynamic" or derived from the theories and ideas of Freud. This theory also recognizes the importance of "behavior" in that we need to also integrate the science of behavior analysis given the obvious effectiveness of this approach in treating autism. Note that these two areas are typically conceived of as diametrically opposed to each other as we have noted previously, but again, to understand autism we need both.

In the present theory of this book or DBT-A, there is a single "pivotal" area that is foundational to all those put forth in PRT and that is the ability to "think about." I am suggesting that pivotal areas such as those noted above are not the core concern (although they are of concern), but rather problems that are derivative of early identification with objects that bars the development of sufficient "thinking about" thinking. For example, we would suggest that a lack of motivation to initiate and engage in a social-communicative encounter is not due to an impaired response-reinforcer contingency, but rather an impaired ability to imagine the thinking and emotion of the potential partner. Self-regulation is impaired because the infant did not or could not yet imagine another person thinking of him or her, so the imagined sense of "self" you and I effortlessly maintain was never generated. Not responding to multiple cues is a function of not seeing the "whole" object or person, and hence one part or cue is focused on excessively. Empathy is impaired because to have empathy, one needs to be able to imagine the other person's state of mind, and the main thrust of DBT-A is that imagination itself is impaired in the child with autism. It's worth noting that the ability to imagine human elements is the most complex form of imagination and could still develop later, after object imagination is in place.

Thus, the basic theoretical ideas of PRT are much different than those of DBT-A, although this difference does not mean that the interventions put forth in PRT might not indirectly lend themselves to what we were doing. On the contrary, PRT has shown good results. But what exactly are the main ideas in terms of PRT treatment? In PRT, the family is intensely involved, and treatment takes place in all the natural environments of the child. When interacting with the child, motivation is fostered by following the child's lead and interests, and providing choices and varied tasks. When the child does initiate or engage in interactive play with the adult, or even makes an approximation of such, the child is reinforced quickly with direct and natural reinforcers. Applied behavior analysis tools are apparent not only in the quick delivery of "reinforcers" and their use with "successive approximations," but also in, for example, the training of verbal behavior and initiations. To encourage skills such as these, parents and teachers are instructed to establish measurable goals based on the known and typical sequence of skills, create a clear opportunity for learning, model frequently, and reinforce immediately. The same type of approach is recommended for other desired behaviors, such as joint attention, pretend play, showing behavior, and alternation of gaze when making a request.

The PRT approach makes sense, employs known behavioral strategies that have been shown to be effective time and again, and focuses on core problem areas for the child with autism. I am a supporter of this approach, and I see it as completely consistent with the intervention approach that we created from DBT-A. However, I think PRT misses the central problem in that it is actually targeting behaviors and problems that are secondary symptoms. The other concern I have heard from parents about PRT (I have given many parents Koegel and LaZebnik's "Overcoming Autism" [2012], which adds more behavioral techniques such as functional behavior analysis and replacement behaviors) is that the ideas and concepts are fine, but parents always ask, "what do I *do*?" By this, they mean that they don't actually know what activities to take part in, and they don't have guidance on what actual play activities to create, initiate, and then encourage. The Meta-play Method that we created is very different from PRT in this respect as well as theory, and lists a range of activities that infants can take part in throughout the day. The implementation of these activities can and should be done consistent with known PRT/behavioral strategies: model, reinforce approximations quickly, teach in all of the child's natural environments, create clear opportunities for learning, etc. The difference with the Meta-play Method is that we focus on a wide range of activities designed solely to: 1) shift identification from objects to people, 2) move from part- to whole-object understanding, 3) foster any and all imagination-based thinking, and 4) increase tolerance of unpredictability over predictability.

To employ the Meta-Play Method, you need to know

something about the behavioral approach as well as behavioral strategies and techniques. Explaining these is far beyond the scope of this book, but the reader is encouraged to access one of the many books or courses on behaviorism to gain a fuller understanding. A good one that I use and refer to often is Mayer, Sulzer-Azaroff, & Wallace's (2012, 2nd Ed.) "Behavior Analysis for Lasting Change." It is also helpful to get hands-on training if possible, so the techniques can and should be practiced under the supervision of a well-trained behaviorist. Fortunately, this is the basic idea behind the growing field of in-home services and supports. Briefly, here is a list of some of the basic concepts and techniques you will need:

1) Positive reinforcement and effective delivery of reinforcers
2) Shaping, chaining, and successive approximations
3) Discrete trial and errorless teaching components and strategies
4) Measuring operationalized behavior goals and tracking change
5) Ignoring and extinguishing non-desired behaviors
6) ABCs of behavior and contingent relations
7) Discriminative stimuli and stimulus control
8) Modeling
9) Generalization

Although certainly not an exhaustive list, these will go a long way toward helping parents, teachers, and others involved in the treatment of the child with autism to implement activities effectively.

Our case study results were encouraging
     I have digressed somewhat from the work we were doing with our initial case study and his family. Getting back to this child

and family, you may be wondering what we did and what happened? Once we got consent for participation from the parents, we educated the entire family on the basic ideas of the theory, and we confirmed the autism diagnosis and severity with the ADOS. The ADOS was scored by a psychologist who was unfamiliar with the purpose of the study. We also collected information on the participant's cognitive functioning, and reviewed some basic behavioral principles such as those noted above. With this information in hand, we began the task of creating a series of possible interventions. This took some time, but we were able to fashion a series of activities based on our theory and we added to these and revised them as the case study progressed. As we worked with our first participant, we found that some of the interventions we came up with were simply of no interest to the toddler, and others needed to be modified or dropped completely. We quickly confirmed that if what you are doing is of no interest to a toddler, you might as well stop because he or she is not going to have anything to do with you. As the study continued, we identified further interventions and were also able to place some of the activities on a continuum of complexity; our first participant was sometimes able to take part in a simpler approximation of our original idea, yet we wondered if the intervention in its original, more complex form might be appropriate for an older child, or one with a less severe presentation. Keeping most everything in our listing, we delineated our categories for ourselves and parents as follows:

Meta-play definition: **Items, interactions, and activities that foster movement on a developmental progression of the creation of meta-cognition, based on object-to-person Dynamic Behavior Theory (DBT-A). Four main concepts include:**

1) **Any process of imagination from object existence to the more abstract human imagining (such as what others are thinking)**
2) **Any engagement that is out of the child's control or a product of (human) <u>un</u>predictability vs. object predictability**
3) **Any activity that fosters movement on the object to human continuum**
4) **Any activity that fosters movement on the part-to-whole continuum**

Our case study toddler made such incredible progress in 6 months that the family, my research assistant, and I were astonished. But of course, this was only one child; perhaps he would have made progress even if we had not intervened. That is always the concern.

In any event, this surprising progress encouraged us to extend our research, so we completed a small-group feasibility study on seven more toddlers, and again achieved good results. Both of these studies were published in well-known journals, and are in the reference section of this book: Woodard et al., 2014; Woodard et al., 2018. Fortunately, we had a pretty well-established set of interventions for the parents to use for this small group study, so we followed the same pattern we used in the case study. We talked with parents about the theory in simple terms until we were reasonably comfortable that they understood it, and also provided some education on basic behavior principles. We provided parents with a manual we created to use as a guide, and tested the toddlers on the ADOS to get some kind of sense of his or her level of autism severity. After this phase, we began visiting the family's home twice a month to introduce the interventions and practices to the parent and the child. Once we got through all of the interventions in the first month or so, we encouraged the parents to modify the interventions as needed, which is why it was essential that the parents fully understand the theory and the ideas behind the various activities we had designed. We found that parents were pretty good at this and often took our ideas and adapted them to new contexts and situations for their child. This flexibility kept things interesting, and helped to engage the child more and more as time went on. After about three months, we reduced our home visit to once a month, because the parents did not need our guidance and support as much. The activities were fun and easy to implement throughout the day, and all members of the family could take part. At the end of the six months of participation, we retested the toddler and found progress similar to that of our case study child. This result didn't happen with all of the participants; one participant did not show an improvement on ADOS severity scoring. But by far the majority of children made progress and their autism symptoms were lessened significantly. This was the first study of its kind to show that you could actually reduce the level of autism severity; up to this point, intervention studies had been able to show some improvements in cognitive levels or adaptive functioning, but the actual reduction of core symptoms of autism remained elusive.

By having a treatment approach such as the Meta-play Method available, and informing parents on how important it is for their child to identify with people, we are in effect suggesting a need to explore, re-ignite, or re-establish the human symbiotic state, and train the child to move towards (or at least tolerate) a human identification process. In many cases, this process is not likely to be pleasant, but the payoff could be great. Recently there has been a call for research that can clearly differentiate between interventions that affect disorder severity, and interventions that are "deeply altering core mechanisms" (Bodfish, 2004). A quick review of the literature shows that the preponderance of treatment outcome indicators is more often adaptive behavior and IQ, rather than measures that focus on the three core symptom domains of

170

autism. Building upon our growing ability to reduce certain behavioral challenges and improve for example, select communicative behaviors with technology, researchers are now being challenged to focus attention on truly desired outcomes, such as "children who spontaneously demonstrate more varied, sustained, and generative ways of interacting with their environments and with others" (p. 324). Bodfish notes that our ability to "promote characteristics like spontaneity, flexibility, and social understanding is likely to depend on our knowledge of the basic behavioral and neurocognitive processes that give rise to and support such personal characteristics" (p. 324).

My message here needs to be clear. If we begin to think differently about the origins and nature of these core, "thinking about" traits and abilities that you and I take for granted, real progress may become possible. If we explore the hypothesis that "spontaneous" behavior derives from apparently unique permutations of the thinking "about" capacity, "flexibility" requires a release from constancy and the ability to think "about" alternatives, and genuine "social understanding" evolves from successful early human identification, we may be able to move away from treating the symptoms of autism and open the door to affecting the core mechanisms that give rise to the developmental trajectory and resulting wide ranging symptoms known as autism. But this is not a simple set of ideas; it is complex and somewhat nebulous, and it takes time and effort to understand, and even more effort to put into practice.

The benefits of having a treatment approach for toddlers with autism symptoms that directly affects human identification is clear, but are there any risks? In short, the answer is "yes." Remember that autism is a "spectrum" disorder, meaning that there is a wide range of presentations of the severity of this disorder. As you move up the spectrum, the symptoms change and hypothetically become less and less severe. That is true to an extent, but persons who are less affected still have significant effects of this disorder that can be debilitating. They have difficulty maintaining relationships, difficulty getting a job and keeping it (unless he or she can find something that involves little contact with others), and often suffer from depression, anxiety and loneliness. It may not be severe autism, but it can be equally devastating. The reason I point this out, is that beyond this severe autism, there are many people who are trying to function with high level ASD. There are others who we are only starting to realize are just over the borderline of autism spectrum disorder (ASD), functioning as "typically developing" people, but they too have difficulties deriving from the spectrum called autism.

I had been waiting for someone to point this out, and sure enough in a recent edition of a popular magazine the *Bottom Line* there was an article on how you may even be in a relationship with someone who has very subtle autism symptoms and not know it, because the presentation is so very difficult to identify. My point is that if you accept the theory I have stated here, autism does not stop at the less severe end of ASD; it is actually a set of traits and symptoms that are permeating all of us to a degree. I wonder how many people reading this book are or know someone who is a representation of what I am talking about: someone who is very rigid in his or her approach to the world, someone who has awkward or just limited social interactions (and the partner, if there is one, covers or compensates for it), someone who is repetitive or has very limited interests in certain areas or topics, or someone who you have noticed, doesn't seem to get your jokes or pick up on the social cues that others seem to understand. These are among the many not-yet-documented effects of autism on our culture.

Remember that "thinking about" is associated with someone's imagination to a great degree. So, beyond social skills, a lesser degree of early identification with objects can also be impairing taking an interest in and understanding others, spontaneous creativity, hypothetical thinking, understanding sub-text or meanings of statements, and flexible problem-solving. When we previously talked about the effects of early autism symptoms on pretend play, we were really talking about the seeds of these later abilities. When children are not staring at a computer or TV screen or are not being fed stimulation on an iPad, they are forced to create their own games, thoughts, images, interactions, and contexts; this activity is essential to normal development. Strangely this same type of cognitive development happens in pretend play, where children are actually encouraged to make a break with reality for a period of time, and then come back to reality when they are done. But for a period of time, the child, typically with another child or two, is in another world of the mind's creation, moving about and interacting with created relationships and contingencies. The importance of this pretend play that starts out simple and then grows into what is known as "socio-dramatic play," cannot be underestimated—and it is one of the events that is lost in the emergence of autism. I would suggest that the cost of this loss is not limited to autism, and that over time we will see its devastating effects in the typically developing population as well in people who cannot interact socially or think "outside the box." With this core cognitive ability impaired, the real victim is a society that has an increasingly limited ability to imagine and create. I don't predict that this loss will happen in an obvious way, but rather in a more insidious manner; years from now we will be looking at our culture and the people in it and we will be asking "What happened?"

The way to avoid this eventuality is clear. **It is essential that we reduce our time on computers, phones, television, and any other screen devices, and force ourselves to increase our uninterrupted social interaction time with each other. Most importantly, this includes our children for whom access to screen devices must be severely limited for a wide variety of**

reasons. Children should no longer be given a device for entertainment. There is value in having to sit at dinner and observe adults interacting, having to create and think on your own without distraction, and having to go for long car rides with nothing to do. What happens as a result? You learn to be with yourself and how to sit and think without being distracted or entertained by something; you day-dream; you imagine. Which leads me to another effect of technology: anxiety. When you have not needed to develop a comfort level with being with yourself with nothing to distract you, having to do so becomes a very scary thing. Think for a moment of being alone in nature, without any devices to turn to. While this should sound calming, it actually will send many younger people in our culture into what my mother would call an "acute conniption." The truth is that anxiety has become rampant in our society, and I am suggesting that this is a "soft sign" of a subtle lack of early human identification and normal early cognitive development. Beyond classic presentations of autism, beyond high-functioning persons with ASD, beyond people who might be considered typically developing but who function with very subtle traits that reflect autism, we have promoted in our society and culture an inability to be comfortable alone and with ourselves, and when you are less able to do this, the outcome is a free-floating, not-sure-where-it-comes-from anxiety.

Our theory has many possible effects beyond the emergence of autism, and perhaps there are some we have not even thought of or considered. Beyond fueling a more typical presentation of the disorder known as autism, there are the effects seen in persons without these more severe symptoms; and persons dealing with very subtle effects but successfully functioning in the larger culture. And then there are people in their 20s and 30s, for whom anxiety is an unwelcome presence in the world, but they can't really identify why or where it came from—it is just there. They have noticed, however, that the anxiety is lessened when they are engaged with a device, which understandably makes it nearly addictive and even the fear of being without it is anxiety-producing. If you don't believe me, ask someone how they would feel if you took away their phone; the idea is nearly unthinkable to most people. Finally, and perhaps most simply, much of the intrinsic enjoyment in life comes from our personal interactions with one another. People must choose to talk, interact, and walk together (without being on the phone). They need to sit down to a meal together. On a first date, they need to know it's OK if they don't always have something to say. They need to go see each other in person instead of texting, and talk at work instead of emailing. It is imperative that as a society we make these choices to re-ignite the practice of social interaction. Why? Because the effects of not doing so are far more devastating than we realize.

Final Thoughts

The actual activities of the Meta-play Method are, as noted previously, only recently derived from the ideas set forth in the Dynamic Behavior Theory of Autism (DBT-A). We have completed a successful case study as well as a small group study on participants with a variety of autism presentations. However, our ideas and interventions await years of research to fully determine efficacy. The reason I have written this book and outlined the activities now is that if I were a parent of a child with autism and someone had an untested idea that might actually help with very little risk of harm, I would want to know about it. At the very least, the activities of the Meta-play Method will give you some fun activities to engage in with your child, and hopefully these will lessen the severity of any autism symptoms that are present. Beyond that, if the base theory is correct, perhaps others will expand on these ideas and come up with even better interventions than those outlined here. I hope that this book has clearly communicated where DBT-A came from, what it is, and how the Meta-play Method activities derive from this theory. I do not want to create false hope in parents of children with autism, but our initial results have been very promising. If they do help in some small way, or if this thinking is a catalyst for another researcher with a better idea that does help treat autism, then I think what has been put forth here has value. My only goal is to offer an idea that while complex, is sensible in hopes of improving the lives of persons affected by this unusual, unique, and debilitating disorder.

References

American Psychiatric Association (2000). *Diagnostic and statistical manual of mental disorders (DSM-IV-TR)*. APA: Washington, DC.

Baillergeon, R., Needham, A., & DeVos, J. (1992). The development of young infants' intuitions about support. *Early Development and Parenting, 1*, 69-78.

Baron-Cohen, S. (1996). *Mindblindness: An essay on autism and theory of mind*. Cambridge, MA: MIT Press.

Baron-Cohen, S. (2002). The extreme male brain theory of autism. In H. Tagler-Flusberg (Ed.), *Neurodevelopmental disorders* (pp. 401-430). MIT Press.

Baron-Cohen, S., Leslie, A. M., & Frith, U. (1985). Does the autistic child have a "theory of mind?" *Cognition, 21*, 37-46.

Bauman, M. L. & Kemper, T. L. (2003). The neuropathology of the autism spectrum disorders: What have we learned? *Novartis Foundation Symposium, 251*, 112-122.

Bernard-Opitz, V., Sriram, N., & Nakhoda-Sapuan, S. (2001). Enhancing social problem solving in children with autism and normal children through computer-assisted instruction. *Journal of Autism and Developmental Disorders, 31(4)*, 377-398.

Blanck, R., & Blanck, G. (1986). *Beyond ego psychology*. New York: Columbia University Press.

Bodfish, J. W. (2004). Treating the core features of autism: Are we there yet? *Mental Retardation and Developmental Disabilities Research Reviews. 10*, 318-326.

178

Bodfish, J. W. (2011). Repetitive behavior in autism: Brain-behavior relationships. Association for Behavior Analysis International (ABAI) Conference Presentation, Washington, DC.

Brown, R., Hobson, R. P., Lee, A., & Stevenson, J. (1997). Are there "autistic-like" features in congenitally blind children? *Journal of Child Psychology and Psychiatry, 38,* 693-703.

Cautela, J., & Groden, J. (1978). *Relaxation: A comprehensive manual for adults, children and children with special needs.* Champaign: Research Press Company.

Celani, G. (2002). Human beings, animals and inanimate objects. *Autism, 6(1),* 93-102.

Centers for Disease Control (2018). Data and Statistics: Autism Spectrum Disorder. Retrieved from www.cdc.gov

Chakrabarti, B., Dudbridge, F., Kent, K., Wheelright, S., Hill-Cawthorne, G., Allison, C., Banerjee-Basu, S., & Baron-Cohen, S. (2009). Genes related to sex steroids, neural growth, and social-emotional behavior are associated with autistic traits, empathy, and Asperger Syndrome. *Autism Research, 2,* 157-177.

Charman, T., & Baron-Cohen, S. (1997). Brief report: Prompted pretend play in autism. *Journal of Autism and Developmental Disorders, 27,* 321-328.

Clifford, S. M., & Dissanayake, C. (2008). The early development of joint attention in infants with autistic disorder using home video observations and parental interview. *Journal of Autism and Developmental Disorders, 38(5),* 791-805.

Courchesne, E., Alshoomoff, N. A., & Townsend, J. (1990). Recent advances in autism. *Current Opinion in Pediatrics, 2*, 685-693.

Dawson, G. (1991). A psychobiological perspective on the early socio-emotional development of children with autism. In D. Cicchetti and S. Toth (Eds.), *Rochester Symposium on Developmental Psychopathology: Volume 3 (pp. 207-234)*. Rochester, NY: University of Rochester.

Dawson, G., & McKissick, F. C. (1984). Self-recognition in autistic children. *Journal of Autism and Developmental Disorders, 14*, 383-394.

DeCasper, A.J., & Spence, M.J. (1986). Prenatal maternal speech influences newborns' perceptions of speech sounds. *Infant Behavior and Development, 9*, 133-150.

Fairbairn, W. R. D. (1941). A revised psychopathology of the psychoses and psychoneuroses. In *An object-relations theory of the personality* (pp. 28-58). New York: Basic Books.

Fairbairn, W. R. D. (1954). Object-relationships and dynamic structure. In *An object-relations theory of the personality* (pp. 137-151). New York: Basic Books.

Falter, C. M., Plaisted, K. C., & Davis, G. (2008). Visuo-spatial processing in autism – Testing the predictions of extreme male brain theory. *Journal of Autism and Developmental Disorders, 38*, 507-515.

Fonagy, P., Gergely, G., Jurist, E., & Target, M. (2002). *Affect regulation, mentalization, and development of the self.* New York: Other Press.

Fonagy, P., & Target, M. (2003). *Psychoanalytic theories.* Whurr Publishers: London.

Forrester-Jones, R., & Broadhurst, S. (2007). *Autism and loss.* Jessica Kingsley Publishers: England.

Frea, W. D. & McNerney, E.R. (2008). Early intensive applied behavior analysis intervention for autism. In J. K. Luiselli, D. C. Russo, W. P. Christian, & S. M. Wilczynski (Eds.), *Effective practices in autism.* Oxford University Press: New York.

Freud, S. (1917). Mourning and melancholia. In *The standard edition of the complete psychological works of Sigmund Freud, Vol. 14* (pp. 237-258). London: Hogarth Press.

Freud, S. (1932). New introductory lectures on psycho-analysis. In *The standard edition of the complete psychological works of Sigmund Freud, Vol. 22* (pp. 58-80). London: Hogarth Press.

Frith, U. (1989). *Autism: Explaining the enigma.* Cambridge, MA: Blackwell.

Gaigg, S. B./, & Bowler, D. M. (2007). Differential fear conditioning in Asperger's Syndrome: Implications for an amygdala theory of autism. *Neuropsychologia, 45(9),* 2125-2134.

Greenberg, J. R., & Mitchell, S. A. (1983). *Object relations in psychoanalytic theory.* Cambridge, MA: Harvard University Press.

Hanlon, P. (2010). Excessive emailing /texting: The newest addiction? *New England Psychologist, 18(6),* 1-12.

Happe, F. (1994). *Autism: An introduction to psychological theory.* Cambridge, MA: Harvard University Press.

Herbert, M. (2005). Autism: A brain disorder, or a disorder that affects the brain? *Clinical Neuropsychiatry, 2, 6,* 354-379.

Hirstein, W., Iverson, P., Ramachandran, V. S. (2001). Autonomic responses of autistic children to people and objects. *Proc. R. Soc. Lond. B, 268,* 1883-1888.

Hobson, P. (2002). *The cradle of thought.* New York: Oxford University Press.

Hobson, P. (2005). Autism and emotion. In F. R. Volkmar, R. Paul, A. Klin, & D. Cohen (Eds.), *Handbook of autism and pervasive developmental disorders, Vol. 1: Diagnosis, development, neurobiology, and behavior* (pp. 406-422). New Jersey: John Wiley & Sons.

Hobson, R. P., Lee, A., & Hobson, J. A. (2010). Personal pronouns and communicative engagement in autism. *Journal of Autism and Developmental Disorders, 40,* 653-664.

Hoek, H. W. (2006). Incidence, prevalence and mortality of anorexia nervosa and other eating disorders. *Current Opinion in Psychiatry, 19(4), 389–394.* doi: 10.1097/01.yco.0000228759.95237.78

Horner, A. J. (1984). Object relations and the developing ego in therapy. New Jersey: Jason Aronson, Inc.

Jacobson, E. (1964). *The self and the object world.* New York: International Universities Press.

Jones, W., Carr, K., & Klin, A. (2008). Absence of preferential looking to the eyes of approaching adults predicts level of social disability in 2-year-old toddlers with autism spectrum disorders. *Archives of General Psychiatry, 65(8),* 946-954.

Kanner, L. (1943). Autistic disturbances of affective contact. *Nervous Child, 2,* 217-250.

Kisilevsky, B. S., Hains, S. M. J., & Low, J. A. (1999). Differential maturation of fetal responses to vibroacoustic stimulation in a high-risk population. *Developmental Science, 2(2),* 234-245.

Klin, A., Lin, D. L., Gorrindo, P., Ramsay, G., & Jones, W. (2009). Two-year-olds with autism orient to nonsocial contingencies rather than biological motion. *Nature, 459* (7244), 257-261.

Knickmeyer, R. C., & Baron-Cohen, S. (2006). Topical review: Fetal testosterone and sex differences in typical social development and in autism. *Journal of Child Neurology, 21,* 825-845.

Koegel, R. L., & Koegel, L. K. (2006). Pivotal response treatments for autism. Baltimore: Paul H. Brooks Publishing.

Kogan, M. D., Blumberg, S. J., Schieve, L.A., Boyle, C.A., Perrin, J. M., Ghandour, R. M., Singh, G. K., Strickland, B. B., Trevathan, E., & Van Dyck, P. C. (2009). Prevalence of parent-reported diagnosis of autism spectrum disorder among children in the US, 2007. *Pediatrics, 124*, 1395-1403.

Kogan et al. (2018). The prevalence of parent-reported autism spectrum disorder among US Children. *Journal of Pediatrics, 142*(6).

Leslie, A. (1987). Pretense and representation: The origins of "Theory of Mind." *Psychological Review, 94*, 412-426.

Lewis, V., & Boucher, J. (1988). Spontaneous, instructed and elicited play in relatively able autistic children. *British Journal of Developmental Psychology*, 6, 325–339.

Lewis, V., & Boucher, J. (1995). Generativity in the play of young people with autism. *Journal of Autism and Developmental Disorders, 25,* 105-122.

Lind, S. E., & Bowler, D. M. (2010). Episodic memory and episodic future thinking in adults with autism. *Journal of Abnormal Psychology, 119(4),* 896-905.

Liss, M., Saulier, C., Fein, D., & Kinsbourne, M. (2006). Sensory and attention abnormalities in autistic spectrum disorders. *Autism, 10(2),* 155-172.

Lopata, C., Thomeer, M. L., Volker, M. A., Toomey, J. A., Nida, R. E., Lee, G., Smerbeck, A. M., & Rodgers, J. D. (2010). RCT of a manualized social treatment for high-functioning autism spectrum disorders. *Journal of Autism and Developmental Disorders, 40,* 1297-1310.

Lord, C., Rutter, M., DiLavore, P. C., & Risi, S. (2002). *Autism Diagnostic Observation Schedule (ADOS).* Western Psychological Services: Los Angeles, CA.

Lovaas, O. I. (1987). Behavioral treatment and normal educational and intellectual functioning in young autistic children. *Journal of Consulting and Clinical Psychology, 55,* 3-9.

Mahler, M., Pine, F., & Bergman, A. (1975). *The psychological birth of the human infant: Symbiosis and individuation.* New York: Basic Books.
Mahler, M. S. (1979a). *The selected papers of Margaret S. Mahler: Volume one.* New York: Jason Aronson.

Mahler, M. S. (1979a). *The selected papers of Margaret S. Mahler: Volume two.* New York: Jason Aronson.

Mann, T., & Walker, P. (2003). Autism and a deficit in broadening the spread of visual attention. *Journal of Child Psychology & Psychiatry & Allied Disciplines, 44,* 274-284.

McDonough, L., Stahmer, A., Schreibman, L., & Thompson, S. J. (1997). Deficits, delays, and distractions: An evaluation of symbolic play and memory in children with autism. *Development and Psychopathology, 9,* 17-41.

Miriam-Webster (2007). Miriam-Webster's medical dictionary. Miriam-Webster, Inc.

Mundy, P., Sigman, M., Ungerer, J., & Sherman, T. (1986). Defining the social deficits of autism: The contribution of non-verbal communication measures. *Journal of Child Psychology and Psychiatry, 27*, 657-669.

Myers, S. M. (2007). The status of pharmacotherapy for autism spectrum disorders. Expert Opinion *Pharmacotherapy*, 8(11): 1579-1603.

Perner, J. (1991). *Understanding the Representational Mind.* Cambridge, MA: The MIT Press.

Piaget, J. (1952). *The origins of intelligence in children.* New York: W. W. Norton & Co.

Piaget, J. (1962). *Play, dreams, and imitation in childhood.* New York: W. W. Norton and Co.

Repacholi, B. M., & Gopnik, A. (1997). Early reasoning about desires: Evidence from 14- and 18-month-olds. *Developmental Psychology, 33*(1), 12-21.

Rogers, S. J., Cook, I., & Meryl, A. (2005). Imitation and play in autism. In F. R. Volkmar, R. Paul, A. Klin, & D. Cohen (Eds.), *Handbook of autism and pervasive developmental disorders, Vol. 1: Diagnosis, development, neurobiology, and behavior* (pp. 382-405). New Jersey: John Wiley & Sons.

Rogers, S. J., & Vismara, L. A. (2008). Evidence-based comprehensive treatments for early autism. *Journal of Clinical and Adolescent Psychology, 37(1)*, 3-38.

Sandler, J. (1987). *Projection, identification, projective identification*. Madison, CT: International Universities Press.

St. Clair, M. (1996). Object relations and self psychology (2nd Ed.). California: Brooks/Cole Publishing Co.

Santangelo, S. L., & Tsatsanis, K. (2006). What is known about autism; Genes, brain, and behavior. *American Journal of Pharmacogenomics, 5*(2), 71-92.

Schafer, R. (1968). *Aspects of internalization*. New York: International Universities Press.

Scherf, K. S., Luna, B., Minshew, N., & Behrmann, M. (2010). Location, location, location: Alterations in the functional topography of face- but not object- or place- related cortex in adolescents with autism. *Frontiers in Human Neuroscience, 4,* (page count 16).

Schreibman, L., Dawson, G., Stahmer, A. C., Landa, R., Rogers, S., McGee, G. G., et al. (2015). Naturalistic developmental behavioral interventions: Empirically validated treatments for autism spectrum disorder. *Journal of Autism and Developmental Disorders*, 45(8), 2411–2428. http://dx.doi.org/10.1007/s10803-015-2407-8.

Stern, D. (1985). *The interpersonal world of the infant.* New York: Basic Books.

Szatmari, P., Jones, M. B., Zwaigenbaum, L., & MacLean, J. E. (1998). Genetics of autism: Overview and new directions. *Journal of Autism and Developmental Disorders, 28*, 351-368.

Terkecki, M. S., & Newcombe, N. S. (2005). How important is the digital divide? The relation of computer and videogame usage to gender differences in mental rotation ability. *Sex Roles, 53(5/6)*, 433-441.

Thornton LM, Mazzeo SE, Bulik CM (2011). The heritability of eating disorders: methods and current findings. *Behavioral Neurobiology of Eating Disorders. Current Topics in Behavioral Neurosciences*. 6. pp. 141–56. doi:10.1007/7854_2010_91

Tick B., Bolton P., Happé F., Rutter M., & Rijsdijk F. (2016). Heritability of autism spectrum disorders: a meta-analysis of twin studies. *Journal of Child Psychology and Psychiatry*, 57(5), 585-95. doi: 10.1111/jcpp.12499.

Tomasello, M. (1999). *The cultural origins of human cognition.* Cambridge: Harvard University Press.

Tomasello, Kruger, & Ratner (1993). Cultural learning. *The Behavioral and Brain Sciences, 16*, 495-552.
Welch, K. C., Lahira, U., Warren, Z., & Sarkar, N. (2010). An approach to the design of socially acceptable robots for children with autism spectrum disorders. *International Journal of Social Robotics, 2(4)*, 391-403.

Willatts, P. (1984). Stages in the development of intentional search by young infants. *Developmental* Wing, L., Gould, J., Yeates, S., & Brierley, L., (1977). Symbolic play in severely mentally retarded and in autistic children. *Journal of Child Psychology and Psychiatry, 18*, 167-178. *Psychology, 20*(3), 389-396.

Wing, L., Gould, J., Yeates, S., & Brierley, L., (1977). Symbolic play in severely mentally retarded and in autistic children. *Journal of Child Psychology and Psychiatry, 18,* 167-178.

Woodward, A.L. (1998). Infants selectively encode the goal object of an actor's reach. *Cognition, 69,* 1–34.

Woodard, C. R., & Van Reet, J. (2011). Object identification and imagination: An alternative to the meta-representational explanation of autism. *Journal of Autism and Developmental Disorders, 41, 214-226.*

Woodard, C. R., Chung, C., & Korn, M. (2014). A pilot study of the meta-play method: a novel play intervention for toddlers with autism. *Journal of Autism,* http://www.hoajonline.com/journals/pdf/2054-992X-1-2.pdf.

Woodard, C. R. & Chung, C. (2018). Feasibility of a play-based intervention set for toddlers with autism. Research in Developmental Disabilities, 80 (September), 24-34. https://doi.org/10.1016/j.ridd.2018.05.010.

Ylisaukko-oja, T., Alarco´n, M., Cantor, R. M., Auranen, M., Vanhala, R., Kempas, E., von Wendt, L., Ja¨rvela¨, I., Geschwind, D. H., & Peltonen, L. (2006). Search for autism loci by combined analysis of autism genetic resource exchange and Finnish families. *Annals of Neurology, 55*(1), 145-155.

189

Zwaigenbaum, L., Bryson, S., Rogers, T., Roberts, W., Brian, J., & Szatmari, P. (2005). Behavioral manifestations of autism in the first year of life. *International Journal of Developmental Neuroscience, 23*, 143-152.

Notes and Thoughts: